Communications
in Computer and Information Science 1851

T0172216

Rationale

The CCIS series is devoted to the publication of proceedings of computer science conferences. Its aim is to efficiently disseminate original research results in informatics in printed and electronic form. While the focus is on publication of peer-reviewed full papers presenting mature work, inclusion of reviewed short papers reporting on work in progress is welcome, too. Besides globally relevant meetings with internationally representative program committees guaranteeing a strict peer-reviewing and paper selection process, conferences run by societies or of high regional or national relevance are also considered for publication.

Topics

The topical scope of CCIS spans the entire spectrum of informatics ranging from foundational topics in the theory of computing to information and communications science and technology and a broad variety of interdisciplinary application fields.

Information for Volume Editors and Authors

Publication in CCIS is free of charge. No royalties are paid, however, we offer registered conference participants temporary free access to the online version of the conference proceedings on SpringerLink (http://link.springer.com) by means of an http referrer from the conference website and/or a number of complimentary printed copies, as specified in the official acceptance email of the event.

CCIS proceedings can be published in time for distribution at conferences or as post-proceedings, and delivered in the form of printed books and/or electronically as USBs and/or e-content licenses for accessing proceedings at SpringerLink. Furthermore, CCIS proceedings are included in the CCIS electronic book series hosted in the SpringerLink digital library at http://link.springer.com/bookseries/7899. Conferences publishing in CCIS are allowed to use Online Conference Service (OCS) for managing the whole proceedings lifecycle (from submission and reviewing to preparing for publication) free of charge.

Publication process

The language of publication is exclusively English. Authors publishing in CCIS have to sign the Springer CCIS copyright transfer form, however, they are free to use their material published in CCIS for substantially changed, more elaborate subsequent publications elsewhere. For the preparation of the camera-ready papers/files, authors have to strictly adhere to the Springer CCIS Authors' Instructions and are strongly encouraged to use the CCIS LaTeX style files or templates.

Abstracting/Indexing

CCIS is abstracted/indexed in DBLP, Google Scholar, EI-Compendex, Mathematical Reviews, SCImago, Scopus. CCIS volumes are also submitted for the inclusion in ISI Proceedings.

How to start

To start the evaluation of your proposal for inclusion in the CCIS series, please send an e-mail to ccis@springer.com.

Paolo Mori · Gabriele Lenzini · Steven Furnell
Editors

Information Systems Security and Privacy

7th International Conference, ICISSP 2021
Virtual Event, February 11–13, 2021, and 8th International
Conference, ICISSP 2022, Virtual Event, February 9–11, 2022
Revised Selected Papers

 Springer

Editors
Paolo Mori
Consiglio Nazionale delle Ricerche
Pisa, Italy

Gabriele Lenzini
University of Luxembourg
Esch-sur-Alzette, Luxembourg

Steven Furnell
University of Nottingham
Nottingham, UK

ISSN 1865-0929   ISSN 1865-0937 (electronic)
Communications in Computer and Information Science
ISBN 978-3-031-37806-5   ISBN 978-3-031-37807-2 (eBook)
https://doi.org/10.1007/978-3-031-37807-2

This Springer imprint is published by the registered company Springer Nature Switzerland AG
The registered company address is: Gewerbestrasse 11, 6330 Cham, Switzerland

Preface

The present book includes extended and revised versions of selected papers from the 7th and 8th International Conferences on Information Systems Security and Privacy (ICISSP 2021 and ICISSP 2022). Both events were held online due to the Covid-19 pandemic. ICISSP 2021 was held from 11–13 February 2021, and ICISSP 2022 from 9–11 February 2022.

ICISSP 2021 received 110 paper submissions from 30 countries, of which 2% are included in this book.

ICISSP 2022 received 107 paper submissions from 32 countries, of which 4% are included in this book.

The papers have been selected based on quality, including comments provided by the program committee members, the session chairs' assessment and the program chairs' global view of all papers in the technical program. The authors of selected papers were invited to submit a revised and extended version of their papers with at least 30% innovative material.

The International Conference on Information Systems Security and Privacy provides a meeting point for researchers and practitioners, addressing information systems' trust, security and privacy challenges from both technological and social perspectives. The conference welcomes papers of either practical or theoretical nature. It is interested in research or applications addressing all aspects of trust, security and privacy and encompassing issues of concern for organisations, individuals and society.

The papers selected in this book contribute to the understanding of relevant trends of current research on Information Systems Security and Privacy, including Vulnerability Analysis and Countermeasures, Threat Awareness Security in IoT and Edge Computing, Security Awareness and Education, Security and Privacy Metrics, Security and Privacy in Cloud and Pervasive Computing, Risk and Reputation Management, Privacy-Enhancing Models and Technologies, Cryptographic Algorithms, Access and Usage Control, Authentication, Privacy and Security Models.

We thank all the authors for their contributions and the reviewers for their help in ensuring the quality of this publication.

February 2021

Paolo Mori
Gabriele Lenzini
Steven Furnell

Organization

Conference Chair

Steven Furnell — University of Nottingham, UK

Program Co-chairs

Paolo Mori — Consiglio Nazionale delle Ricerche, Italy
Gabriele Lenzini — University of Luxembourg, Luxembourg

Program Committee

Served in 2021

Alessandro Barenghi	Polytechnic University of Milan, Italy
Andrea De Salve	CNR, Italy
Andrea Saracino	Consiglio Nazionale delle Ricerche - Istituto di Informatica e Telematica, Italy
Ashok Kumar Das	International Institute of Information Technology, Hyderabad, India
Christoph Kerschbaumer	Mozilla Corporation, USA
David Sanchez	Universitat Rovira i Virgili, Spain
Eleonora Losiouk	University of Padua, Italy
Elisavet Konstantinou	University of the Aegean, Greece
Hossein Saiedian	University of Kansas, USA
Hung-Min Sun	National Tsing Hua University, Taiwan, Republic of China
Ismail Butun	KTH Royal Institute of Technology, Sweden
Mathias Fischer	University of Hamburg, Germany
Matt Bishop	University of California Davis, USA
Michael Scott	Certivox Ltd., Ireland
Mingcong Deng	Tokyo University of Agriculture and Technology, Japan
Nadira Lammari	Conservatoire National des Arts et Métiers, France
Rakesh Verma	University of Houston, USA

Feng Cheng	Hasso-Plattner-Institute at University of Potsdam, Germany
Fernando Pereñiguez	University Centre of Defence, Spanish Air Force Academy, Spain
Flamina Luccio	Università Ca' Foscari Venezia, Italy
Francesco Buccafurri	University of Reggio Calabria, Italy
Francesco Mercaldo	National Research Council of Italy (CNR), Italy
Fu-Hau Hsu	National Central University, Taiwan, Republic of China
Günther Pernul	University of Regensburg, Germany
Gaurav Sharma	Université libre de Bruxelles, Belgium
Gianluca Lax	University of Reggio Calabria, Italy
Gianpiero Costantino	Consiglio Nazionale delle Ricerche, Italy
Gilles Guette	University of Rennes, France
Hervé Chabanne	Idemia & Télécom Paris, France
Hugo Barbosa	Lusofona University, Portugal
Hung-Yu Chien	National Chi Nan University, Taiwan, Republic of China
Ilaria Matteucci	Istituto di Informatica e Telematica, CNR, Italy
Kallol Karmakar	University of Newcastle, Australia
Karen Renaud	University of Strathclyde, UK
Konstantinos Limniotis	Hellenic Data Protection Authority, Greece
Letterio Galletta	IMT Institute for Advanced Studies Lucca, Italy
Lorenzo De Carli	Worcester Polytechnic Institute, USA
Luigi Catuogno	Università degli Studi di Salerno, Italy
Mario Alvim	Federal University of Minas Gerais (UFMG), Brazil
Mariusz Jakubowski	Microsoft Research, USA
Mark Gondree	Sonoma State University, USA
Mauricio Papa	University of Tulsa, USA
Montserrat Batet	Universitat Rovira i Virgili, Spain
Morteza Amini	Sharif University of Technology, Iran
Nader Safa	University of Wolverhampton, UK
Neil Rowe	Naval Postgraduate School, USA
Nicola Zannone	Eindhoven University of Technology, The Netherlands
Nikolaos Pitropakis	Edinburgh Napier University, UK
Nilanjan Sen	Western Illinois University, USA
Panayiotis Kotzanikolaou	University of Piraeus, Greece
Pierpaolo Degano	Università di Pisa, Italy
Raylin Tso	National Chengchi University, Taiwan, Republic of China
Sashank Narain	University of Massachusetts Lowell, USA

Shambhu Upadhyaya	University at Buffalo, USA
Shujun Li	University of Kent, UK
Silvio Ranise	Fondazione Bruno Kessler, Italy
Stelvio Cimato	Università degli Studi di Milano - Crema, Italy
Stjepan Picek	TU Delft, The Netherlands
Weizhi Meng	Technical University of Denmark, Denmark
Wolfgang Reif	University of Augsburg, Germany
Yin Pan	Rochester Institute of Technology, USA
Zubair Khattak	Mohi-Ud-Din Islamic University, Pakistan

Additional Reviewers

Served in 2021

Tahir Ahmad	Fondazione Bruno Kessler, Italy
Loenzo Ceragioli	Università di Pisa, Italy
Salimeh Dashti	Fondazione Bruno Kessler, Italy
Vincenzo De Angelis	University of Reggio Calabria, Italy
Cecilia Labrini	University of Reggio Calabria, Italy
Lara Mauri	Università degli Studi di Milano, Italy
Majid Mollaeefar	Fondazione Bruno Kessler, Italy
Jens Wettlaufer	Universität Hamburg, Germany
Florian Wilkens	Universität Hamburg, Germany

Served in 2022

Rudra Baksi	Illinois State University, USA
Stefano Berlato	University of Genoa, Italy
Duy Dang	RMIT Vietnam, Vietnam
Marco De Vincenzi	IIT-CNR, Italy
Daniel dos Santos	Forescout, The Netherlands

Served in 2021 and 2022

Sebastian Ramacher	AIT Austrian Institute of Technology, Austria

Invited Speakers

2021

Adrian Perrig	ETH Zürich, Switzerland
Matteo Maffei	TU Wien, Austria
Karen Renaud	University of Strathclyde, UK

2022

Awais Rashid	University of Bristol, UK
Pierangela Samarati	Università degli Studi di Milano, Italy
Norman Sadeh	Carnegie Mellon University, USA

Contents

ICScope: Detecting and Measuring Vulnerable ICS Devices Exposed on the Internet

Yixiong Wu[1], Shangru Song[1], Jianwei Zhuge[1,2(✉)], Tingting Yin[1], Tianyi Li[3], Junmin Zhu[4], Guannan Guo[5], Yue Liu[6], and Jianju Hu[7]

[1] Institute for Network Science and Cyberspace / BNRist, Tsinghua University, Beijing, China
zhugejw@tsinghua.edu.cn
[2] Zhongguancun Laboratory, Beijing, China
[3] Peking University, Beijing, China
[4] Shanghai Jiao Tong University, Shanghai, China
[5] School of Computer Science and Technology,
University of Science and Technology of China, Hefei, China
[6] QiAnXin Technology Research Institute, Beijing, China
[7] Siemens Ltd, Beijing, China

Abstract. Industrial Control Systems (ICS) play an important role in modern Industrial manufacturing and city life, as well as an critical attack surface. However, many ICS devices are deployed without proper security consideration, such as being exposed to the public Internet without protection. Furthermore, the ICS devices are hardly updated or patched due to the stability requirements. Therefore, the Internet-accessible ICS devices generally have publicly known vulnerabilities, which makes them fragile victims. In this work, we propose a method to measure the security status of Internet-facing ICS devices in a passive way and develop a prototype ICScope. With ICScope, we can find vulnerable devices without actively scanning the ICS device, which may have negative effects on their normal operation. ICScope collects device information from multiple public search engines like Shodan, gets vulnerability information from vulnerability databases like NVD, and matches them according to the vendors, products, and versions. ICScope can deal with the incomplete device data collected from the search engines and has taken the honeypots into consideration. We use ICScope to launch a comprehensive evaluation of the ICS devices exposed to the Internet between Dec 2019 and Jan 2020, including 466K IPs. The result shows that 49.58% of Internet-facing ICS devices have at least one publicly known vulnerability. We also observed a downward trend in the number of ICS devices and their vulnerable percentage during our measurement spanning 1.5 years.

Keywords: Internet-facing ICS devices · Passive vulnerability assessment · Device search engine

---

A earlier version appeared at the 7th International Conference on Information Systems Security and Privacy (ICISSP 2021) Yixiong Wu and Shangru Song contribute equally to this works.

1   Introduction

Industrial Control System(ICS) plays an important role in the infrastructure of modern cities. To electronically manage tasks efficiently, Industrial devices with computing and communication capabilities are used in nearly every critical infrastructure and industrial sector such as the manufacturing, energy, transportation, etc. ICS is original designed to provide communication between devices in isolated operation LANs. As a result, security mechanisms are not sufficiently considered to ensure the security of the communication. ICS devices are rarely updated or upgraded during maintenance to avoid issues such as cost and compatibility. The average time taken to fix ICS vulnerabilities is much longer than others. Due to the requirements of data collection and remote maintenance, industrial control systems are connected to the Internet, which exposes the ICS devices to an unsafe environment and finally leads to potential risks of cyber-attacks [12]. Takayuki Sasaki [18] has detected real attacks on geographically distributed infrastructures, which change critical parameters.

For securing industrial control systems, previous works have focused on finding the exposed ICS devices, including active scanning-based [9, 13, 14, 16, 18, 23], search engine-based [10, 15, 16, 20], and traffic-based [21]. Both Mirian et al. [14] and Feng et al. [9] have performed active scanning on the Internet to discover the exposed ICS devices. However, they focus on the exposed ICS devices rather than the vulnerable, exposed ICS devices. Takayuki Sasaki [18] works on the insecure ICS remote management devices. But their approach can only discover exposed ICS devices with Web User Interface (WebUI). These active scanning-based approaches need to send packets to industrial control systems, which may affect the stability of industrial control systems. ShoVAT [10] and Scout [15] both use search engines to detect vulnerable services on the Internet, such as HTTP and IMAP. Considering the inconsistent banner format between common services and ICS devices, these approaches cannot be applied to ICS devices. Samtani et al. [16] only focus on the vulnerable Supervisory control and data acquisition (SCADA) on the Internet. To the best of our knowledge, there is no work that reveals the security status of Internet-facing ICS devices in the whole public IP address space. This knowledge gap should be filled to secure industrial control systems, which motivates us to carry out this study.

Compared with using vulnerability scanners like Zmap and Nessus (*Active Mode*), the search engine-based vulnerability assessment (*Passive Mode*) is more suitable for identifying ICS devices' vulnerabilities. Discovering the vulnerable ICS devices on the Internet by search engines is non-trivial, and several challenges need to be addressed ahead: *1)* The banners returned by search engines are fragmented: Each search engine's capabilities and scanning nodes are different, resulting in inconsistent banner format and potential data missing. *2)* There are industrial honeypots on the Internet to detect ICS threats. *3)* It's not easy to detect the ICS device's vulnerabilities without any interaction.

In this work, we propose a passive vulnerability assessment system based on device search engines. For ethical consideration, our system ICScope uses passive mode to avoid intrusive behaviors. To address the first challenge, we design the data enrichment module. In this module, we build a device fingerprint database that helps us to determine the vendor and product information based on the specific fields in banners.

Furthermore, we also integrate the device information extracted from multiple search engines to enrich the incomplete device information. To address the second challenge, we regard an ICS device as a honeypot when the device information extracted from multiple search engines is inconsistent. And we also utilize some non-interaction features, such as ISP, ICS honeypot fingerprinting. For the third challenge, the vulnerability association module builds vulnerability trees to identify each ICS device's vulnerabilities.

We have implemented ICScope and measured the security status of exposed ICS devices in the whole public IP address space. Between Dec 2019 and Jan 2020, we used ICScope to discover 270,283 exposed ICS devices. There are 21,578 ICS honeypots among these exposed ICS devices detected by ICScope. Excluding these ICS honeypots, there are only 106,382 ICS devices that can extract complete ICS device entries by ICScope. Finally, ICScope has discovered 52,739 vulnerable ICS devices (about 49.58%) among ICS devices with complete info. Most detected vulnerabilities are high or critical and can be exploited remotely with few restrictions. ICScope can be used to measure the impact of the 0day vulnerabilities. We found that a 0day vulnerability can affect 3,999 exposed ICS devices. We also utilized ICScope to conduct a long-time measurement from June 2020 to Dec 2021. Despite the high vulnerable percentage of exposed ICS devices, the number of exposed ICS devices and their vulnerable percentage have decreased slowly.

Contribution. The contributions are listed as follows:

1. We design a new passive vulnerability assessment tool named ICScope, for automated Internet-facing ICS devices vulnerability detection.
2. We utilize ICScope to discover the exposed ICS devices and assess their security status. We find that 49.58% of exposed ICS devices with complete entries are vulnerable.
3. We proposed a non-interaction ICS honeypot detection approach. By this methodology, we have detected about 21.5K honeypots (about 7.98%) on our datasets.

Our results reveal the severe and considerable security risks faced by ICS devices in the current cyberspace. At the end of the paper, we discuss the mitigation measures against this security threat. A earlier version [24] has been published in the 7th International Conference on Information Systems Security and Privacy (ICISSP 2021). In this extended version, we have added a new measurement spanning from Jan 2021 to Dec 2021 to show a more comprehensive view of exposed ICS devices' security status. During this new measurement, we observed that the vulnerable percentage of exposed ICS devices with complete entries had increased at least 6%, and the average vulnerable percentage was about 60%. However, neither the number of exposed ICS devices nor the number of vulnerable ICS devices have a growing trending. We also add Sect. 2 to introduce the background of the industrial control system and device search engines.

2 Background and Related Works

2.1 Industrial Control System

Industrial Control Systems refers to the automatic control systems composed of computers and industrial control components, including Supervisory Control and Data

Acquisition (SCADA), Distributed Control System (DCS), and Programmable Logic Controller (PLC), etc. ICS is wildly used in critical infrastructures including nuclear power plants, communication systems, sewage-processing plants, etc. It's also very common in factories and building management systems. Due to the critical role of ICS facilities for the country and daily life, they are always aimed targets for cyber-criminals, and even APT groups. Attackers targeting the ICS system may be state sponsored or represent the benefits of some cybercrime organizations. And attacks towards ICS are usually well organized and highly damaging.

ICS protocols are important languages for communication between ICS applications and devices. It is an indispensable part of remote data monitoring. With the development of information technology and the demand for real-time and reliability of plant level monitoring, Ethernet is widely introduced to industrial control network. TCP/IP or ISO standard encapsulation is used in data transmission. However, the necessary measures to ensure the safety of users, such as encryption and authentication is not well considered at the beginning of the ICS protocol design. More importantly, ICS protocols are always command oriented, function oriented and polling answered. An attacker can get arbitrary data access to target device as long as the device is exposed to the Internet and the attacker knows the certain protocol used by the device.

Even though the product vendor of a ICS device release security patch, factories and plants may choose not to apply the patch. This is because the installation of these patches means the change of origin environment, which has uncertain impact to the safety, operability or reliability of the ICS. In order to eliminate these negative effects as much as possible, engineers needs to test the compatibility of the patches in virtual test environment. If the patches pass the tests, they could be deployed during the routine shutdown maintenance, usually once or twice a year. However, for some critical systems that need to run continuously, patches cannot be deployed because there is no downtime. Because of the particularity of working environment of ICS, the life cycle of ICS vulnerabilities is much longer than other types of vulnerabilities.

2.2   Device Search Engines

Cyberspace is a large address space that links billions of Internet devices, and the applications and services held on these devices are countless. Different from traditional search engine like google, cyberspace search engines focus on how many devices and services are exposed to the Internet. The granularity of device search engine detection is generally until the device or service is identified, without paying attention to its further content information.

During scanning, the device search engine will traverse the entire IPv4 address space. For each IP, the device search engine interacts with a specific port according to the detection script to detect whether the port is open or not. If device search engine found an open port, it then performs banner grabbing. Banner is a simple text or binary message that a server send to a client during the connection. It is considered as the service fingerprints to identify the opening services. Device search engines establish TCP/UDP connections with open ports and get the banner information from the application running on ports. Then they compare the banner with the banner fingerprints in their database to identify the services as well as the version numbers, product vendors, product names and so on.

There are several well known device search engines such as Shodan, Censys, FOFA and SiNan. Shodan [3] is widely known as an Internet-wide scanning project founded in 2009 by Matherly. It is also one of the earliest device search engine. Censys [1] is a project developed by a research group from the University of Michigan. It was released in 2015. FOFA [2] was developed by Baimaohui Inc in 2015 which is well known and widely used in China. SiNan is an internal device search engine newly developed by QiAnXin in 2018. We obtained ICS data from them through academic cooperation. We use these four device search engines to identify ICS devices that exposed directly to Internet.

2.3 Related Work

Passive Vulnerability Assessment in Cyberspace. Passive vulnerability assessment is an eco-friendly and resource-conserving research method for large-scale security measurement towards Cyber-Space. B Genge et al. [10] propose ShoVAT, which is the first Shodan-based passive vulnerability assessment tool. The CPE-based vulnerability matching technique used by ShoVAT depends heavily on the quality of its CPE dictionary. Jamie O'Hare et al [15] improve the previous work and propose Scout to implement passive vulnerability assessment of HTTP services on the Internet. Scout focuses on the accuracy of vulnerability matching compared with ShoVAT, and Scout's results are more practical than the scanning result of OpenVAS. However, neither of them is suitable for the industrial control scenario. Because their matching techniques depend on the quality of the banners returned by search engines, the banners are commonly incomplete in ICS. We use our data enrichment module to alleviate this problem. Moreover, the honeypot issue has rarely been considered in previous works on passive vulnerability assessment. ICScope tries to solve this problem to increase the accuracy of vulnerability detection.

Online ICS Device Discovery. Previous works on discovering online ICS devices are always a hot topic on ICS security. Mirian et al. [14] scan the public IPv4 address space to discover online ICS devices through extending ZMap [7] to support four ICS protocols. Feng et al. [9] developed their ICS device discovery system to conduct ICS device discovery based on investigating 17 industrial control protocols. Although they have tried to minimize the number of probing packets, their systems still need to interact with target devices. Meanwhile, Sasaki et al. [17] implement device discovery through Web GUI interface, but their focus is limited to ICS remote management devices. Thomas et al. [21] discovered online ICS devices by passive scanning, but the scope and type of scanning nodes are limited. Using multiple search engines, ICScope can discover online ICS devices without any communication interactions and better tolerate the limitation of scanning nodes.

ICS Honeypot Detection. The honeypots in ICS security are often used for ICS threat analysis [14,19,22]. There are few works focused on ICS honeypot detection. Feng et al. [9] propose a learning model to determine the probability of an ICS honeypot and a heuristic algorithm to verify it with the minimum number of probing packets. However, both the learning model and the algorithm are based on the probing packets. There is no probing packet with ICS devices in ICScope, because the ICS honeypot detection method used in ICScope is based on non-interaction features.

3 Motivation and Challenges

3.1 Motivation

The risk of Internet-facing ICS devices is a long-standing issue. Most existing research focuses on what devices have been exposed to the Internet or the malicious behavior of attackers [8]. Researchers conduct vulnerability assessments for Internet-facing ICS devices [13,16]. Furthermore, these researches are usually limited in scope and scale. More importantly, their methods cannot avoid intrusive behaviors.

In this paper, we conduct a large-scale empirical measurement to provide a more comprehensive and holistic view of Internet-facing ICS devices' security status. By integrating data from multiple search engines, we obtain more comprehensive Internet-facing ICS devices and conduct passive vulnerability assessments on them. We further analyze the vulnerable ICS devices and related vulnerabilities in multiple dimensions, such as geolocation distribution and vulnerability ratio. To decrease false positives, we also perform a non-interaction ICS honeypot detection, while the previous vulnerability assessment works not.

3.2 Technical Challenges

There are three main challenges with designing a passive vulnerability assessment system.

Incomplete Banners. The banner returned by the device search engines may not contain complete device information. For example, the different banners for the same ICS device are respectively returned by Shodan and FOFA (see Fig. 1a and Fig. 1b). Compared with Shodan, the FOFA's banner lacks the $Basic\ Firmware$ information, which used to extract version information. Moreover, neither of them contains vendor and product information. Existing research that reconstructs CPE names from banners is limited by the lack of device information. Fortunately, we observe that the capabilities of the device search engines are different, and part of device information can be identified by a specific field in ICS protocol. Based on this observation, we attempt to extract the complete device information from the banners returned by multiple device search engines on the basis of ICS protocol features. For the ICS device in Fig. 1, we extract its version from the Shodan banner. And We obtain its vendor and product from the SIEMENS online shop through the article number found in the banner.

Honeypot Detection. Industrial honeypots are wildly used for the detection of industrial control security threats [19]. The device search engines also add honeypots to the query results to monitor their abuse by attackers. Previous research [9] utilizing network fingerprinting technology [4] is not working here because of the lack of interaction. We use the non-interaction features to detect ICS honeypots, such as device inconsistencies in different search engines and the fingerprints of open-source ICS honeypots.

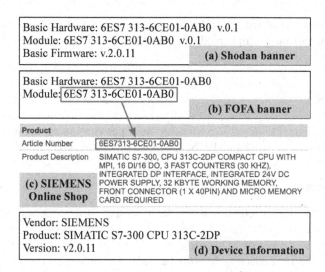

Fig. 1. Device information for SIMATIC S7-300 with banners returned by Shodan and FOFA [24].

Associate Vulnerabilities. Previous works [10,15] use the most similar CPE name reconstructed from banner to find possible vulnerabilities. However, this method is limited to ICS. First, some ICS devices might have more than one CPE name, while others do not. For instance, the device's CPE name in Fig. 1 can be `cpe:/h:siemens:simatic_s7-300_cpu:2.0.11` or `cpe:/h:siemens:simatic_s7-300_cpu_313:2.0.11`. Second, the CPE data utilized to to to identify the impact range of a vulnerability in the National Vulnerability Database (NVD) is

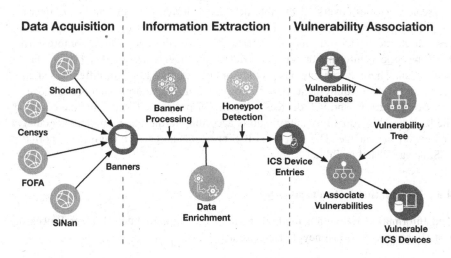

Fig. 2. Architecture of the ICScope [24].

overstated or underestimated [5]. Instead of reconstructing the CPE name, we construct vulnerability trees from multiple public vulnerability libraries and use them to associate vulnerabilities.

4   ICScope

We propose a method to detect ICS vulnerabilities passively in an automatic way and develop a prototype system named ICScope based on this method.

4.1   Architecture

Figure 2 shows the architecture of ICScope. It consists of three parts, i.e., the Data Acquisition module (DA), the Information Extraction module (IE), and the Vulnerability Association module (VA). The DA module is responsible for collecting Internet-facing ICS device data via the Application Programming Interface (API) of search engines (Sect. 4.2). The IE module will further extract the key features (e.g. vendor names, product names, and versions) of the devices from the row data collected by DA (Sect. 4.3). The data from ICS honeypots will also be filtered by the IE module(Sect. 4.3). Lastly, the VA constructs the public vulnerability information into tree structures and searches the potential vulnerabilities for devices according to their key features extracted by DA (Sect. 4.4).

4.2   Data Acquisition

The DA carefully constructs search statements to abundant comprehensive devices from different databases. ICScope uses the public devices search engines to collect device information without intrusively interacting with the ICS devices. However, none of the search engines covers all the Internet-facing devices. According to the measurement [11] published by Guo et al., integrating the result of different search engines can enrich the device information dataset. To make the result more comprehensive, ICScope collects information for four different search engines: Shodan, Censys, FOFA, and SiNan. These search engines provide public search APIs with different searching grammar for data requirement. For example, in FOFA[1], the users should use the string protocol:s7 to find ICS devices using the S7 protocol. The DA module constructs the legal and high quality search requests according to the search engines' documents and expert knowledge. The supported ICS protocols and search engines supported by ICScope are listed in Table 1.

4.3   Information Extraction

The Information Extraction module includes three submodules: Banner Processing, Data Enrichment, and Honeypot Detection.

---

[1] https://fofa.so/.

Table 1. Protocols supported by ICScope. ✓: supported by device search engine; △: enriched by ICScope [24].

Protocol Name	Device Search Engines				Enrich
	Shodan	Censys	FOFA	SiNan	
Modbus	✓	✓	✓	✓	–
Siemens S7	✓	✓	✓	✓	△
DNP3	✓	✓	✓	✓	–
Niagara Fox	✓	✓	✓	✓	△
BACnet	✓	✓	✓	✓	△
EtherNet/IP	✓	–	✓	✓	△
GE-SRTP	✓	–	✓	✓	–
HART-IP	✓	–	✓	✓	–
PCWorx	✓	–	✓	✓	△
MELSEC-Q	✓	–	✓	✓	–
OMRON FINS	✓	–	✓	✓	△
Crimson v3	✓	–	✓	✓	–
CoDeSys	✓	–	✓	✓	△
IEC 60870-5-104	✓	–	✓	✓	–
ProConOS	✓	–	✓	✓	–
VertX Edge	–	–	✓	✓	△
Moxa NPort	–	–	✓	✓	–
Lantronix UDP	–	–	✓	✓	–
Koyo DirectNet	–	–	–	✓	–
HollySys MACS	–	–	–	✓	–
Proficy-webspace	–	–	–	✓	–
Siemens License	–	–	–	✓	–
Total	15	5	18	22	8

Banner Processing. In this step, ICScope extracts the key features of the ICS devices from the raw data returned by the online device search engines. The key features include two parts: vulnerability-related identifiers and extra information used in Data Enrichment. The first part can be formally represented as a tuple $\langle vendor, product, version \rangle$. The second part mainly includes the device-specific identifiers used for recognizing the same device among different data sources, for example, the product ID.

Data Enrichment. Many banners collected from the search engines are incomplete, which makes it hard to associate the device and the vulnerability information. To make the measurement more comprehensive, ICScope completes their information with the following three strategies.

Data Enrichment Based on Industrial Control Protocol. For some ICS protocols, we can identify device information by special attributes returned in the banners. For the BACnet protocol, we can identify the vendor name through the numerical "vendor identifier" field. And some proprietary protocols are only used by several vendors, e.g., SIEMENS for S7 protocol. Based on these observations, we build mappings between identifiers and device information to help ICScope supplement the missing information.

Data Enrichment Based on Fingerprint Database. The values of special fields in some ICS protocols have fixed formats. As shown in Fig. 1, the article number 6ES7

313-6CE01-0AB0, which is in the Module filed of the S7 protocol, is the identifier of SIMATIC S7-300. Inspired by this observation, we build the fingerprint database for ICS devices.

Data Enrichment Based on Multiple Search Engines. ICScope combines the data from different search engine results to complete the device information. Different search engines focus on different protocol fields in ICS protocol. Given the banner data in Fig. 1 as an example, FOFA and Shodan return different banners of the same device using the protocol SIMATIC S70300 (i.e., the banner from FOFA is lack of the firmware version). Therefore, ICScope completes each device information according to the information from four search engines: Shodan [3], Censys [6], FOFA [2], and SiNan[2].

Honeypot Detection. Online honeypots bring noise to the measurement results. To make the follow-up analysis result more accurate, ICScope filters honeypots out of the dataset according to the following three characteristics.

Data Inconsistency. In industrial practice, the ICS devices are hardly upgraded or replaced. Therefore, even though the online search engines probe the ICS devices at different times, the devices' information they collect is usually consistent. Based on this observation, ICScope cross-compares the device information from different search engines and regards the device with inconsistent information as honeypots. The device using multiple protocols at the same time is also considered as violating the data inconsistency rule and is classified as honey-pots. This method may also remove some ICS gateway devices from the database. For these devices, we can recognize them via non-ICS protocol characteristics like HTTP information. We leave this optimization as future work.

Public Honeypots Fingerprints. ICScope builds a honeypot fingerprint dataset based on the open-source industrial honeypot information. The information used in the fingerprint includes default configuration, prompt information, device-specific identifiers like MAC, etc. With these fingerprints, ICScope can further exclude the honeypots from the dataset.

ISP Services. Developers usually use Internet service providers (ISP) to deploy ICS honeypots. However, there are no ISP services available for ICS deployment. Thus, ICScope regards the devices as honeypot if they use IP addresses belonging to the Cloud service providers.

---

[2] An internal device search engine newly developed by QiAnXin, china in 2018.

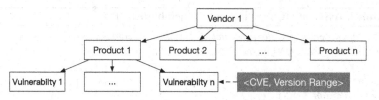

Fig. 3. Data structure used to store vulnerabilities (Vulnerability Tree). Green color denotes the information stored on the leaf. [24] (Color figure online).

4.4 Vulnerability Association

Vulnerability Data Source. ICScope collects comprehensive vulnerability information from multiple vulnerability databases: CNNVD (China National Vulnerability Database of Information Security), SecurityFocus, and NVD (National Vulnerability Database). In addition to the basic vulnerability information, ICScope uses exploit databases to figure out whether the vulnerability has public exploit methods. The exploit databases it supports include PacketStorm, SecurityFocus, and Exploit-DB.

Vulnerability Tree. ICScope uses multi-forked tree forest to represent the vulnerability properties. The vulnerabilities in the same tree affect the same vendor. The structure of the vulnerability tree is shown in Fig. 3. Each vulnerability node has a depth of three. The root node of the tree is the `vendor`. The child nodes of the vendor are `product`. Each `product` dominates multiple `vulnerability` nodes. The `vulnerability` nodes store their affecting version range of the product.

Associate Vulnerabilities. ICScope uses the device information tuple $\langle vendor,$ $product, version \rangle$ extracted by the `IE` module to search their related vulnerabilities in the vulnerability tree. The search process is formalized in the Algorithm 1. The `sim_lookup()` function in the algorithm is a fuzzy search method. ICScope uses it to match the vendors and products, which avoids the false negative caused by differences in the expression. If a device falls into the affecting version range of a vulnerability, ICScope adds the CVE number of the vulnerability to the device's vulnerability set (R_{cve}). With the vulnerability tree, ICScope can match the devices and their vulnerabilities with a minimized comparison time.

Algorithm 1. Associate ICS device with vulnerabilities.

Input: ICS device entry $\langle vendor, product, version \rangle$, Vulnerability Tree($VT$)
Output: a set of possible CVE names (R_{cve})
   $R_{cve} \leftarrow \{\}$
   $vt\_vendors \leftarrow$ all root nodes of VT
   for each $vt\_vendor \in vt\_vendors$ **do**
     if $sim\_lookup(vendor, vt\_vendor)$ **then**
        $vt\_products \leftarrow$ all sub-nodes of vt_vendor in VT
        for each $vt\_product \in vt\_products$ **do**
          if $sim\_lookup(product, vt\_product)$ **then**
             $vt\_vuls \leftarrow$ all leaves of $vt\_product$ in VT
             for each $\langle cve, versionRange \rangle \in vt\_vuls$ **do**
               if $match(version, versionRange)$ **then**
                  $R_{cve} \leftarrow R_{cve} + cve$
               end if
             end for
          end if
        end for
     end if
   end for

5 Demystifying Internet-Facing ICS Devices Security Status

We analyze the overall security status of the Internet-facing ICS devices with ICScope. In this section, we'll introduce the dataset collected by ICScope and the analysis result in detail. In addition, we evaluated vulnerability detection ability of ICScope by comparing it with Shodan.

5.1 Data Collection

ICScope builds two datasets: the device information database and vulnerability database. As introduced in Sect. 4.2, ICScope collects device information from four public device search engines: Censys, SiNan, Shodan, and FOFA. Starting from Dec 2019, end to Jan 2020, ICScope collects 219.238k, 85.531k, 76.489k, and 78.363k device information from them respectively, including 270.283k independent IPs. In order to reveal the security status trend, we ran ICScope between June 2020 and Dec 2021 to discover the vulnerable ICS devices exposed in the Internet. The data spanning one and half years consists of two parts. The first part is data collected by ICScope every three months from June 2020 to December 2020, and the second is collected by ICScope every month from Jan 2021 to Dec 2021.

For vulnerability data, ICScope collects them from five public vulnerability databases: SecurityFocus, NVD, CNNVD, PacketStorm, and Exploit-DB. After removing the overlap data from them, ICScope collects 286.269k vulnerability

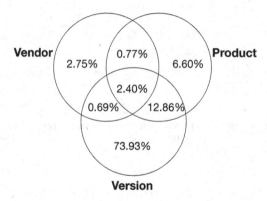

Fig. 4. Attribution-distribution of inconsistent ICS devices. The three circles represent the percentage of devices with *vendor*, *product*, and *version* inconsistency among all inconsistent devices. [24].

5.2   Accuracy Validation

ICScope collects device information and recognizes honeypots in a passive way. To validate the accuracy of its results, we compared them with some ground truth.

For vulnerability discovery, we report the 319 vulnerable ICS devices discovered by ICScope to the relevant Computer Emergency Response Team (CERT) in our country. Till now, the CERT team has analyzed 59 of them and confirmed all of these devices are marked correctly. This proves the result of ICScope is highly accurate. We are planning to cooperate with the CERT team to detect vulnerable ICS devices with ICScope.

We evaluate the accuracy of honeypot detection by comparing it with the honeypot detection service provided by Shodan[3]. In the device dataset build by ICScope, Shodan marks 55 IPs of them as honeypots, among which ICScope recognizes 52 honeypots. We manually analyzed the other three IPs, Two of them do not have the complete information needed for vulnerability matching. The other one does not show honeypot-like suspicious behaviors.

5.3   The Honeypots in Internet-facing ICS Devices

ICScope recognizes 21.578k honeypots among the 270.283k IPs it collects. All of the three strategies introduced in Sect. 4.3 contribute to the result. For more details, the multi-source comparison finds 18.428k honeypots (85.4%), the ISP-based method finds 3.653k (16.93%), and the fingerprint finds 3.653k (16.93%). Some honeypots are detected by multiple methods.

5.4   The Advantage of Multiple Device Search Engines

Honeypot Detection. Since the ICS devices are rarely updated or modified, the devices that different search engines label with different information are likely to be honeypots. Most of the differences are version-related. Figures 4 shows the proportion of the

---

[3] https://honeyscore.shodan.io/.

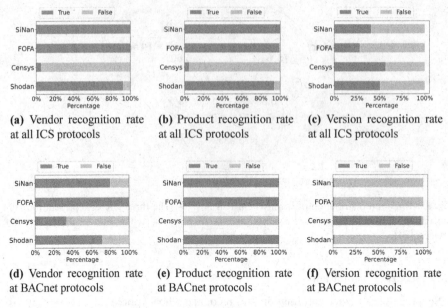

Fig. 5. Recognition rate of different attributions.

version, product, and vendor each account for. Some of the differences are caused by normal firmware iteration. To avoid false positives, ICScope only marks the device as honeypots that have all three attributes inconsistent among different search engines, i.e., the overlapping field accounts for 2.40% in Fig. 4.

Data Enrichment. In Sect. 3.2, we introduced that one challenge of the passive device information collection is that the search engines can not provide complete information for each device. ICScope addresses this challenge by merging the data from different engines to enrich the device information. The search engines have various abilities in the different data fields. Figure 5a, Fig. 5b, and Fig. 5c shows the recognization rate among all ICS protocols for each search engine. It shows that all of the search engines have defects in identifying versions. Censys is limited in detecting vendors and products, but better in identifying versions than the other three ones. Using the devices using the BACnet protocol as an example (Fig. 5d, 5e, 5f)), ICScope gets the vendor and product information from FOFA, Shodan, and SiNan, and complete the version information with CenSys.

5.5   The ICS Devices Affected by Public Vulnerabilities

As shown in Table 3, only 9 out of 22 ICS protocols can extract complete device entries. For these ICS protocols, we obtained about 215k ICS devices using device search engines and detected about 15k ICS honeypots in them. Among these exposed ICS devices, we got about 106k (about 53.10%) ICS devices with complete device entries. Using ICScope, we found about 52k (about 49.58%) ICS devices affected by one or more vulnerabilities. Figure 6 shows the percentage of vulnerable ICS devices in different protocols.

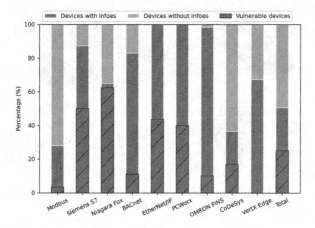

Fig. 6. Vulnerable device percentage at protocol-level.

Table 2. Statistics result of vulnerable devices. [24].

Protocol Name	Vulnerable	Devices	Vulnerable Percentage
Modbus	3461	28600	12.10%
Siemens S7	4400	7663	57.42%
Niagara Fox	35669	37060	96.25%
BACnet	1918	14405	13.31%
EtherNet/IP	4006	9171	43.68%
PCWorx	1444	3610	40.00%
OMRON FINS	208	2032	10.24%
CoDeSys	1633	3526	46.31%
VertX Edge	0	315	0.00%
Total	52739	106382	49.58%

Devices: refers to total number of ICS devices with complete vendor, product and version information.

Protocol-Distribution. Table 2 shows that about 50% of Internet-facing ICS devices are vulnerable and at risk of being compromised. 6 out of 10 ICS protocols have a vulnerability percentage of over 40%. In particular, the Niagara Fox protocol is close to 100%. There is no vulnerable ICS devices for Vertx Edge protocol. The reason is that the only remote code execution vulnerability that affected the HID VertX/Edge devices in the public vulnerability databases cannot find its impact scope on the Internet.

Geo-distribution. To understand the reason behind the high vulnerable percentage, we investigate the correlation between spatial location and vulnerable ICS device distribution. As shown in Fig. 7, We can find vulnerable ICS devices in the vast majority of countries around the world. Furthermore, the top five countries are the United States, Italy, Canada, France, and Spain. The number of vulnerable ICS devices in the United States is over 10 thousand, which accounts for 40.11% of all vulnerable ICS devices exposed on the Internet. Among the six continents, the vulnerable percentage of exposed ICS devices in North America is at the top, with an overall rate of 39.48%. The rest are Australia (20.99%), South America (20.23%), Europe (19.93%), Asia (11.66%)

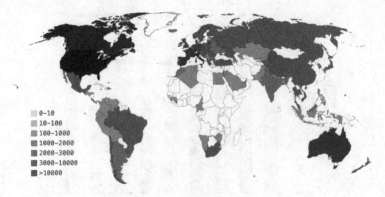

Fig. 7. Geo-distribution of vulnerable ICS devices [24].

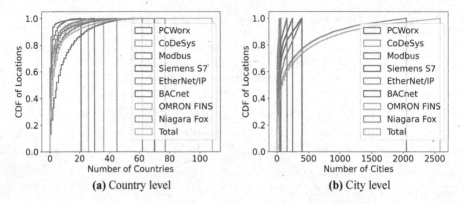

(a) Country level   **(b)** City level

Fig. 8. Location distribution of vulnerable ICS devices [24].

and Africa (9.15%). As shown in Fig. 8a, the ICS protocols have a similar distribution characteristic. The top countries own most of the vulnerable ICS devices. For example, more than 90% of the vulnerable ICS devices with the Niagara Fox protocol can be found within the top 10 countries. As shown in Fig. 8b, there is also a long-tail effect on the vulnerable ICS devices at the city level. Among 9 ICS protocols, the Niagara Fox protocol has the most extensive coverage. More than 43% of the Niagara Fox vulnerable devices are located in the top 50 cities, 60% of the Niagara Fox are in the top 134 cities.

5.6   The Statistics of ICS Vulnerabilities

In this section, we study the statistics of the ICS vulnerabilities mentioned above. We find that the number of unique vulnerabilities which affect the vulnerable ICS devices exposed on the Internet is only 207. We will show the impact scope, CVSSv3 score, and life cycle of ICS vulnerabilities at the protocols level.

Top Vulnerabilities in Different ICS Protocols. Table 3 shows the top 5 ICS vulnerabilities of different ICS protocols and the corresponding number of exposed ICS devices

Table 3. Top 5 vulnerabilities in different ICS protocols [24].

Modbus		Siemens S7		BACnet	
CVE	Numbers	CVE	Numbers	CVE	Numbers
CVE-2015-7937	3095	CVE-2017-2680	4384	CVE-2019-18249	1770
CVE-2015-6461	3077	CVE-2017-2681	4384	CVE-2016-4495	37
CVE-2015-6462	3077	CVE-2017-12741	4337	CVE-2016-3155	36
CVE-2018-7241	2462	CVE-2019-10936	4246	CVE-2018-7779	27
CVE-2018-7242	2462	CVE-2018-13815	3021	CVE-2018-7795	25
Total vul num: 22		Total vul num: 56		Total vul num: 93	
PCWorx		OMRON FINS		CoDeSys	
CVE	Numbers	CVE	Numbers	CVE	Numbers
CVE-2019-9201	1444	CVE-2015-0987	208	CVE-2014-0760	1633
CVE-2019-10953	605	CVE-2015-1015	195	CVE-2014-0769	1633
Total vul num: 2		Total vul num: 2		Total vul num: 2	
EtherNet/IP		Niagara Fox			
CVE	Numbers	CVE	Numbers		
CVE-2017-7898	3147	CVE-2017-16744	35669		
CVE-2017-7899	3147	CVE-2017-16748	35669		
CVE-2017-7901	3147	CVE-2018-18985	35669		
CVE-2017-7902	3147	–	–		
CVE-2017-7903	3147	–	–		
Total vul num: 29		Total vul num: 3			

Numbers: refers to the number of devices affected by the vulnerabilities.

affected by them. We can find that more than half of the industrial control protocols have less than five vulnerabilities. For example, the three vulnerabilities of the Niagara Fox protocol affect about 96.25% of all Niagara Fox ICS devices with complete information. Measures should be taken to fix or mitigate them as soon as possible.

The Severity of ICS Vulnerabilities in Different ICS Protocols. The CVSSv3 can help us to assess the severity of ICS vulnerabilities. About 22.22% (46 out of 207) of ICS vulnerabilities have CVSSv3 score because of the release time of CVSSv3. Figure 9a

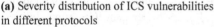

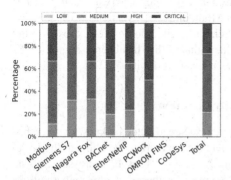

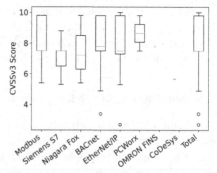

(a) Severity distribution of ICS vulnerabilities in different protocols

(b) Average score and outliers of ICS vulnerabilities in different protocols

Fig. 9. Severity of ICS vulnerabilities [24].

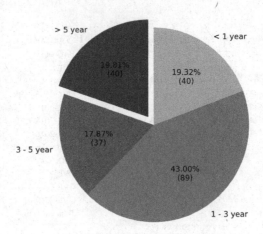

Fig. 10. Vulnerabilities Existing Time.

shows the severity of the ICS vulnerabilities. We observed that more than 60% of ICS vulnerabilities are at the high or critical level. As show in Fig. 9b, The average CVSSv3 scores revolve around 7.5, and most vulnerabilities' scores are spread across the 7.5–10 spectrum. Among the ICS vulnerabilities, 69.23% are remotely exploitable, 74.52% do not require any special conditions, and 66.35% could be executed without authorization.

The Timeline of ICS Vulnerabilities in Different ICS Protocols. As shown in Fig. 10, most of the ICS vulnerabilities are disclosed within three years. Among these vulnerabilities, we can find 40 (19.32%) public exploits on the Internet, which indicates that these corresponding affected devices are in highly dangerous state.

5.7   The ICS Devices Affected by 0day Vulnerabilities

ICScope can be used to assess the impact of 0day vulnerabilities. In this section, we will show that the assessment result of a 0day vulnerabilities. There are four products affected by our 0day vulnerabilities, such as Modicon M580 (version $\leq$ 3.10). Using ICScope, we observed that there are 3,999 Schneider Electric devices exposed to the Internet are affected by this vulnerability. This vulnerability has been assigned CVE-2020-7543 and the vendor had released a new firmware to fix it.

5.8   Comparison with Shodan Vulnerability Detection

Shodan supports detecting whether the target devices are affected by known vulnerabilities. For the exposed ICS devices with complete device entries, we utilized Shodan to discover the vulnerabilities which affect them. Among the 106k IP addresses, Shodan regard 3,472 (about 3.26%) as vulnerable devices. Furthermore, the vulnerabilities returned by Shodan are all Web-based vulnerabilities rather than ICS vulnerabilities. By contrast, ICScope finds that 52,739 (about 49.58%) ICS devices are vulnerable. As for ICS vulnerability detection, ICScope performs better than Shodan.

5.9   The Security Status Trend of Exposed and Vulnerable ICS Devices

To better understand the security status of ICS devices, we conducted a measurement spanning from June 2020 to Dec 2021 (1.5 years) to show the security status trend of the Internet-facing ICS devices. This measurement consists of two parts. From June 2020 to Dec 2020, we ran ICScope per three months, and collected 46,489/38,466/37,027 vulnerable ICS devices, respectively. During this experiment, ICScope obtains device information from Shodan, Cenysys, FOFA, and SiNan. Considering cost and data quality, ICScope obtained ICS devices' information from Shodan and FOFA on the following experiment. We utilized ICScope to discover the vulnerable ICS devices on the Internet every month between Jan 2021 and Dec 2021. We collected 168,618 Internet-facing ICS devices in this experiment and detected 17,359 ICS honeypots (about 10.29%). Among the remaining exposed ICS devices, we find 117,777 ICS devices with complete device entries. Using ICScope, we identified 72,469 exposed ICS devices that are vulnerable. Next, we will show the security status trend behind these data.

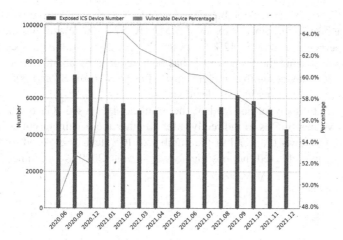

Fig. 11. Security status trending of exposed ICS devices in total.

Figure 11 shows the number of exposed ICS devices with complete device entries and their vulnerable percentages at different times. The vulnerable percentage is above 49.59% for almost all the measurement results. However, the number of exposed ICS devices and their vulnerable percentages are declining. From Jan 2021, the vulnerable percentage dropped from a high of 64.07% to 55.90%. It seems that people had taken some measures to secure the exposed ICS devices.

In order to understand the reasoning behind it, we analyze the measurement results at the ICS protocol granularity. Figure 12a shows the changes in exposed ICS devices' numbers, and Fig. 12b reveals the trend of the vulnerable percentage in exposed ICS devices. As shown in Fig. 12a, there is a slowly decreasing trend in the number of vulnerable ICS devices for most ICS protocols during our measurement period. In contrast, the vulnerable percentages at ICS protocol granularity remain stable. Compared with

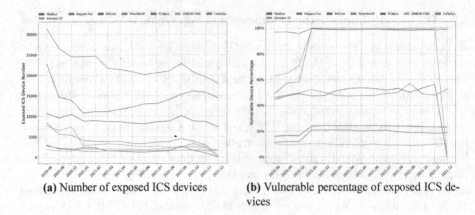

(a) Number of exposed ICS devices

(b) Vulnerable percentage of exposed ICS devices

Fig. 12. Security status trending of exposed ICS devices at different ICS protocols.

the data in Sect. 5.5, the vulnerable rates in some ICS protocols have increased. For example, the growing number of exposed SIMATIC S7-1200 devices has increased the vulnerable percentage from 57.42% to about 99%. By contrast, the number of vulnerable ICS devices using the S7 protocols has been reduced by about 1,600. We cannot discover any ICS devices with complete entries for the Siemens S7 and PCWorx protocols on Dec 2021, resulting in a sudden decrease.

Next, we will analyze the trend of the number of exposed ICS devices affected by different vulnerabilities to indirectly infer whether these vulnerabilities have been fixed. Figure 13 shows the trend of the number of ICS devices exposed to the top 10 vulnerabilities that affected the most devices from June 2020 to December 2021. The

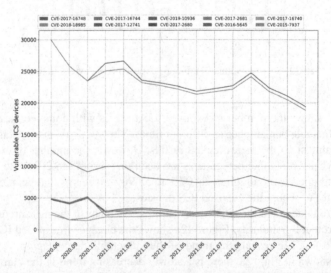

Fig. 13. Trending in the number of vulnerable ICS devices affected by different CVEs.

overall trend of the number of affected devices shows a slight decrease, but it is not particularly significant. This may be due to the particularity of ICS devices, which leads to a longer repair cycle. However, there are also some vulnerabilities, such as CVE-2015-7937, where the number of devices affected remains largely unchanged. This may be due to the fact that the affected devices by these vulnerabilities vary in type and usage. For example, the three vulnerabilities CVE-2017-16748, CVE-2018-18985, and CVE-2017-16744, which show a clear decreasing trend, affect the Niagara Framework developed by Tridium, which is a software update and relatively easier to deploy. However, CVE-2015-7937 affects Schneider Electric Modicon M340 PLC BMXNOx and BMXPx devices, which require firmware updates to fix, and M340 devices are commonly used in the process industry, renewable energy applications, and other industries where device updates are slow.

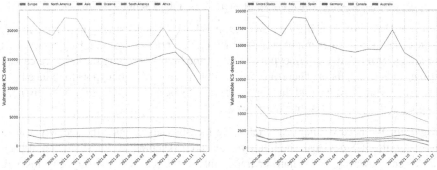

(a) Trending in the number of vulnerable ICS devices in different continents

(b) Trending in the number of vulnerable ICS devices in different countries

Fig. 14. Security status trending of vulnerable ICS devices in different geographical locations.

Finally, we analyze the changing trends of Internet-facing ICS devices with vulnerabilities from the perspective of geographic location attributes. Figure 14a shows the trend of the number of vulnerable ICS devices found on different continents. And Fig. 14b shows the trend from the top 5 countries with the highest number of vulnerable ICS devices. It can be observed a more obvious downward trend in Europe and North America, but other continents remain basically unchanged. This is mainly because the countries showing a clear downward trend are from these two continents. The United States, Italy, and Spain are the top three in terms of the number of vulnerable ICS devices reduced during the observation cycle.

6   Discussion

Ethical Considerations. From an ethical point of view, we conduct our measurements in a completely passive mode to avoid any potential harm. The data used for ICScope doesn't contain sensitive data, and the public search engines provide data which is publicly available. However, since the vulnerable ICS devices are still unfixed, we cannot directly publish our datasets and vulnerable ICS devices with more than 52K. Rather, we report vulnerable ICS devices in our country to related CERT, and we also attempt to contact several vendors.

Limitations. First of all, the above experiment results show only a subset of the security state of Internet-facing ICS devices. The real situation should be more severe. This is a limitation because it is hard or impossible to obtain all Internet-facing ICS devices through search engines, and not all ICS devices can be extracted complete information. Second, although we obtain vulnerable Internet-facing ICS devices, we still do not confirm whether there are any defenses on these devices. This is because ICScope identifies vulnerabilities based on version, not proof of concept (PoC). Third, the supporting ICS protocols of ICScope are constrained to the search engines' capabilities. ICScope supports an ICS protocol only when its banners contain key fields. Fourth, the lack of raw probing packets makes it more difficult to extract device information or detect ICS honeypots, because some information in search engine generated banners may be lost.

Honeypot Detection. It is difficult to detect ICS honeypots accurately in passive mode. For instance, ICS devices might share one IP through port forwarding. However, this is also a fingerprint to detect honeypots. Without the help of probing packets, we cannot distinguish between them. Therefore, we treat them all as ICS honeypots to reduce false positives. Fortunately, we find that this problem may be corrected by the data from non-ICS port, and we leave it as our future work.

Mitigation. We need to take some defensive measures to mitigate the security risk of Internet-facing ICS devices. The intuitive measure is keeping the latest version of each ICS device. However, this is hard or impossible in the real ICS environment. Instead, we can take the following defensive measures:

Add Firewall Policy. Through adding firewall to limit source IP and destination port, we can prevent the attack from accessing the vulnerable ICS devices.

Network Isolation. Isolate the ICS devices requiring Internet connection from those that do not need to protect the attacker from accessing the vulnerable devices.

7 Conclusion

ICS devices are important infrastructure for modern industrial production and cities. With the remote control demands, more and more ICS devices are accessible over the internet. However, most of them are not protected with proper security mitigation. We develop ICScope to reveal the security status of the Interface-faced ICS devices by analyzing their public vulnerabilities. ICScope finds that 49.58% out of the ICS devices with complete device information (i.e., product, vendor, and version) have at least one known vulnerability. Most of the vulnerable devices are using CoDeSys, Niagara Fox, and PCWorx protocols. Surprisingly, 96.25% of the devices using Niagara Fox are vulnerable. The ICS vulnerabilities are disruptive. 60% of them have high or critical level severity. During our long-time measurement, The number of exposed ICS devices and their vulnerable percentage show a slowly decreasing trend. Nevertheless, due to the stability consideration, the ICS devices are rarely updated or patched. It should also be noticed that we keep conservative during the whole analyzing process, which means the conclusion we summarized in this paper is more optimistic than the real situation. Based on these observations, we suggest the ICS operation engineers should deploy some security mitigation like firewalls and strict network isolation to protect the ICS system.

Acknowledgements. This work was supported in part by National Natural Science Foundation of China under Grant U1936121. We would like to thank all anonymous reviewers for their valuable feedback that greatly helped us improve this paper. Besides, we would like to thank Yuxiang Lu, Zhenbang Ma, Yu Wang, for their helping in our work.

References

1. Censys. https://censys.io/
2. Fofa. https://fofa.so/
3. Shodan. https://shodan.io/
4. Comer, D.E., Lin, J.C.: Probing TCP implementations. In: Usenix Summer, pp. 245–255 (1994)
5. Dong, Y., Guo, W., Chen, Y., Xing, X., Zhang, Y., Wang, G.: Towards the detection of inconsistencies in public security vulnerability reports. In: 28th {USENIX} Security Symposium ({USENIX} Security 19), pp. 869–885 (2019)
6. Durumeric, Z., Adrian, D., Mirian, A., Bailey, M., Halderman, J.A.: A search engine backed by internet-wide scanning. In: Proceedings of the 22nd ACM SIGSAC Conference on Computer and Communications Security, pp. 542–553. ACM (2015)
7. Durumeric, Z., Wustrow, E., Halderman, J.A.: ZMAP: fast internet-wide scanning and its security applications. In: 22nd {USENIX} Security Symposium ({USENIX} Security 13), pp. 605–620 (2013)
8. Fachkha, C., Bou-Harb, E., Keliris, A., Memon, N.D., Ahamad, M.: Internet-scale probing of CPS: inference, characterization and orchestration analysis. In: NDSS (2017)
9. Feng, X., Li, Q., Wang, H., Sun, L.: Characterizing industrial control system devices on the internet. In: 2016 IEEE 24th International Conference on Network Protocols (ICNP), pp. 1–10. IEEE (2016)
10. Genge, B., Enăchescu, C.: Shovat: Shodan-based vulnerability assessment tool for internet-facing services. Secur. Commun. Netw. **9**(15), 2696–2714 (2016)
11. Guo, G., Zhuge, J., Yang, M., Zhou, G., Wu, Y.: A survey of industrial control system devices on the internet. In: 2018 International Conference on Internet of Things, Embedded Systems and Communications (IINTEC), pp. 197–202. IEEE (2018)
12. Kesler, B.: The vulnerability of nuclear facilities to cyber attack; strategic insights: Spring (2010)
13. Leverett, É., Wightman, R.: Vulnerability inheritance programmable logic controllers. In: Proceedings of the Second International Symposium on Research in Grey-Hat Hacking (2013)
14. Mirian, A., et al.: An internet-wide view of ICS devices. In: 2016 14th Annual Conference on Privacy, Security and Trust (PST), pp. 96–103. IEEE (2016)
15. O'Hare, J., Macfarlane, R., Lo, O.: Identifying vulnerabilities using internet-wide scanning data. In: 2019 IEEE 12th International Conference on Global Security, Safety and Sustainability (ICGS3), pp. 1–10. IEEE (2019)
16. Samtani, S., Yu, S., Zhu, H., Patton, M., Chen, H.: Identifying Scada vulnerabilities using passive and active vulnerability assessment techniques. In: 2016 IEEE Conference on Intelligence and Security Informatics (ISI), pp. 25–30. IEEE (2016)

17. Sasaki, T., Fujita, A., Ganan, C., van Eeten, M., Yoshioka, K., Matsumoto, T.: Exposed infrastructures: Discovery, attacks and remediation of insecure ICS remote management devices. In: 2022 2022 IEEE Symposium on Security and Privacy (SP) (SP), pp. 1308–1325. IEEE Computer Society, Los Alamitos, CA, USA, May 2022. https://doi.org/10.1109/SP46214.2022.00076, https://doi.ieeecomputersociety.org/10.1109/SP46214.2022.00076

18. Sasaki, T., Fujita, A., Gañán, C.H., van Eeten, M., Yoshioka, K., Matsumoto, T.: Exposed infrastructures: discovery, attacks and remediation of insecure ICS remote management devices. In: 43rd IEEE Symposium on Security and Privacy, SP 2022, San Francisco, CA, USA, 22–26 May 2022, pp. 2379–2396. IEEE (2022). https://doi.org/10.1109/SP46214.2022.9833730

19. Serbanescu, A.V., Obermeier, S., Yu, D.Y.: ICS threat analysis using a large-scale honeynet. In: 3rd International Symposium for ICS & SCADA Cyber Security Research 2015 (ICS-CSR 2015) 3, pp. 20–30 (2015)

20. Simon, K., Moucha, C., Keller, J.: Contactless vulnerability analysis using Google and Shodan. J. Univers. Comput. Sci. 23(4), 404–430 (2017). http://www.jucs.org/jucs_23_4/contactless_vulnerability_analysis_using

21. Thomas, A.M., Marali, M., Reddy, L.: Identification of assets in industrial control systems using passive scanning. In: Pandian, A.P., Fernando, X., Haoxiang, W. (eds.) Computer Networks, Big Data and IoT. LNDECT, vol. 117, pp. 269–283. Springer Nature Singapore, Singapore (2022). https://doi.org/10.1007/978-981-19-0898-9_21

22. Vasilomanolakis, E., Srinivasa, S., Cordero, C.G., Mühlhäuser, M.: Multi-stage attack detection and signature generation with ICS honeypots. In: NOMS 2016–2016 IEEE/IFIP Network Operations and Management Symposium, pp. 1227–1232. IEEE (2016)

23. Williams, R., McMahon, E., Samtani, S., Patton, M.W., Chen, H.: Identifying vulnerabilities of consumer internet of things (IoT) devices: A scalable approach. In: 2017 IEEE International Conference on Intelligence and Security Informatics, ISI 2017, Beijing, China, 22–24 July 2017, pp. 179–181. IEEE (2017). https://doi.org/10.1109/ISI.2017.8004904

24. Wu, Y., et al.: From exposed to exploited: drawing the picture of industrial control systems security status in the internet age. In: ICISSP, pp. 237–248 (2021)

Zero Update Encryption Adjustment on Encrypted Database Queries

Maryam Almarwani[1,2(✉)], Boris Konev[1], and Alexei Lisitsa[1]

[1] Department of Computer Science, University of Liverpool, Liverpool, UK
{M.almarwani,Konev,A.Lisitsa}@liverpool.ac.uk
[2] Department of Computer Science, Taibah University, Medina, Saudi Arabia
mmmarwani@taibahu.edu.sa

Abstract. Multilayered encryption of data is used in the popular approaches to querying encrypted databases, such as [34]. The encryption level of a particular data element can be adjusted to provide a controllable leak of the information about data required for a query execution. Zero Update (ZU) Encryption Adjustment is part of broader Release-Aware Encryption Adjustment (RAEA) schema and seeks to avoid unnecessary data leakage into data storage and reduce numerous communications rounds for multiple query executions. In this paper, we examine Zero Update Encryption Adjustment [11] on the client side. We investigate ZU's performance by constructing specific queries and analysing performance factors such as increasing the number of expressions conditions in a query or documents matching the results as well as utilising indexes. In addition, we evaluated the ZU using a variety of database models. The performance of ZU is compared using three different databases: MongoDB, OrientDB, and MySQL. The results demonstrate the efficiency of Zero Update Encryption Adjustment, which allows for efficient querying over encrypted data on the client-side while maintaining security and performance trade-offs.

Keywords: Adjustment techniques · Zero update encryption adjustment · MongoDB · Client-side adjustment

1 Introduction

Individuals and organisations increasingly depend on external servers to efficiently and consistently store and transmit information. Although data outsourcing benefits data management and accessibility, it also establishes new privacy and security concerns. If data owners no longer have direct control over external servers, they may find their confidentiality and integrity compromised. The sensitive amount of information gathered and stored on other servers increases the requirement for efficient data protection. Individuals and organisations need to protect their sensitive information from unauthorised external users and malicious insiders. While the external server often ensures data availability, it should not have access to the data it stores or have the opportunity to leak sensitive information. Consequently, security is required against honest-but-curious servers that handle data honestly but may lack the data owner's trust. Assuring efficient and practical data protection in such situations represents a challenging problem that requires the development of effective techniques that allow data owners to specify data

P. Mori et al. (Eds.): ICISSP 2021/ICISSP 2022, CCIS 1851, pp. 25–47, 2023.
https://doi.org/10.1007/978-3-031-37807-2_2

privacy requirements and technologies for enforcing such obligations via data storage and processing. Encrypting all data addresses the privacy problem and also provides the advantages of outsourced storage. Although a certain level of privacy can be achieved, performance and scalability may be an issue, as commonly the encrypted data should be decrypted before processing. Concerns relating to data privacy and confidentiality and processing in outsourcing scenarios (e.g., CryptDB [34], RAEA [9, 10]) have prompted the proposals for querying encrypted data directly without full decryption. Depending on the query an adjustment of the encryption level of data may still be required and various adjustment policies provided with different trade-offs between data privacy and query efficiency. Although Release-Aware Encryption Adjustment (RAEA) [9, 10] had less leakage than Simple Encryption Adjustment (SEA) [34] (see Sect. 2.2 for more details), in [10], ideas were provided to further limit leakage on RAEA using Update-Aware Adjustments approaches (Global Update, Necessary Update, Zero-Update), with the best outcome being the Zero-Update adjustment, which does not leak any information. However, while performing the adjustment processes on the server-side, Zero Update Encryption Adjustment demands that the secret keys are passed to the server, which raises security concerns in the event of abuse. As a consequence, it is proposed in [10] for the maximum level of security, the adjustment processing is performed on the client side, even though this has an impact on performance due to the rounds of communications between client and server. For example, ZeroDB is one of the studies that follows this method of not exposing information to the database and processing the query on the client-side. However, the outsourced servers are unable to process the data in certain database engines, such as MongoDB [38], or due to security concerns; any procedures requiring decrypted data must be performed on the client-side. Egorov et al. [24, 29] introduced ZeroDB, a database that uses B+-trees to allow clients to conduct equality and range searches. It employs an interactive approach that requires many two way rounds and therefore is inefficient in terms of data scalability. The paper [11] introduced Zero Update Encryption Adjustment, a policy that conducts equality and range searches using adjustment techniques. It does not require two way rounds and is therefore effective for data scalability. Therefore, Update-Aware Adjustments were examined in [11] on OrientDB [19] which allows to process data in both sides, in order to identify the impact of adjustment processing on the server and client sides. This paper, on the other hand, concentrates on Zero Update Encryption Adjustment, which provides a high level of security in the MangoDB environment, which only supports the client-side and tests it on SEA, next to RAEA, which has been pre-tested on OrientDB. The main goal of this paper is to investigate the Zero Update-aware techniques proposed by the paper [11] for ensuring the confidentiality of outsourced data and preventing data leakage to the server. This paper expands [10, 11] as follows:

– We establish Zero Update (ZU) Encryption Adjustment effectively on MongoDB.
– We define variable factors that impact Zero Update Encryption Adjustment via MongoDB between various data sizes, and database types capable of performing a Zero Update Encryption Adjustment on them.
– We define a Zero Update Encryption Adjustment with and without indexing feature.
– We demonstrate the efficacy of Zero Update Encryption Adjustment under existing adjustment techniques (SEA,RAEA).

– Furthermore, we conduct evaluations and experiments to show the efficacy and feasibility of Zero Update Encryption Adjustment.

This paper is organized as follows: Preliminaries is described in Sect. 2. Zero Update Encryption Adjustment case study under RAEA and SEA are introduced in Sect. 3. Zero Update Encryption Adjustment Assessment are addressed, including Variable Assessment and Comparing with different Databases in Sect. 4. Section 5 presents Computational Load of Zero Update Encryption Adjustment based on the utilised definitions. Performance and security analysis are reported in Sect. 6. Zero Update Encryption Adjustment is tested in Sect. 7. Related works are listed in Sect. 2. Summary is drawn in the final Sect. 9.

2   Preliminaries

2.1   Onion and Multi-layers Encryption

In onion layers encryption, as described in [11], each piece of data is encrypted with at least one "onion." Figure 1 [34] shows that each onion is made up of layers of increasingly secure types of encryption such as RND (Random) layer [34] $\preceq$ Deterministic encryption (DET) [34] $\preceq$ Order-Preserving encryption (OPE) [16] $\preceq$ PLAIN. Each layer of an onion can handle a different set of computation. Each encryption type releases some information about encrypted values, and the information inclusion induces generally a *partial* order on the encryption types [9].

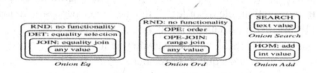

Fig. 1. Onion Layers Encryption [34].

The **outer layers** of onion layers encryption provide higher level of protection, but limited or none operations support (i.e. RND), while **inner layers** allow for more operations at the cost of reduced security (i.e. DET, OPE). These arrangements lead to the necessity of the encryption level adjustments depending on a query to be executed. A proxy, as shown in Fig. 2, is a component in CryptDB-like systems between the Database Server and the application. It adjusts data that has been encrypted using Onion layers to perform queries on encrypted data. The proxy, operates as follows: it obtains a query from a user application and adjusts the data; it rewrites the query by

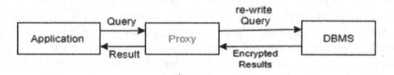

Fig. 2. Workflow of Querying over Onion Layers Encrypted data [10].

replacing constants with encrypted ones and sends it to the database; it decrypts the returned results before transmitting them to the application.

2.2 Encryption Adjustment Policies

In this section [11], we will study at the encryption adjustment policies for the Document Database. The first is a simple encryption adjustment policy proposed in the original CryptDB [34] system for relational data model. The second is the Release-Aware In-Out Encryption Adjustment policy.

2.3 Simple Encryption Adjustment

Simple Encryption Adjustment policy (SEA) follows very simple principles. According to SEA, *before* an execution of a query Q such as in example below, the encryption levels of *all* values of *all* fields f occurring in Q have to be adjusted to the encryption levels $S_Q(f)$.

```
Q: db.collection.find($condition:{f1: $op1 v1,....fn: $opn vn});
```

The query Q itself has to be rewritten into its "encrypted" version Q^*: all plain values of all fields f in Q have to be replaced by encrypted $S_Q(f)$ values.

```
Q*: db.collection.find($condition:{f1:$op1 E_SQ_f1(v1),
...fn: $opn E_SQ_fn(vn)});
```

Such defined policy operates *inwards* - starting with the maximum security level (or minimum wrt to information release order $\preceq$) it adjusts the encryption to lower security (higher wrt $\preceq$) levels for some data elements fields. SEA policy was first proposed for relational databases in [34]. SEA can be extended naturally to the *outward* mode too: after SEA applied inwards, and a query is executed, the encryption of *all* adjusted values of *all* fields f occurring in Q have to be restored to the outer layer of maximal security.

2.4 Release-Aware Encryption Adjustment

Release-Aware In-Out Encryption Adjustment (RAEA) [10] is a dynamic adjustment policy that combines several simple but powerful ideas. Firstly, the adjustment steps are interlaced with the query execution, which reduces the exposure of the data at lower protection encryption layers. Secondly, adjustment is done not only from outer to inner layers, but also in the opposite direction to restore a higher level of data protection after the query execution. Thirdly, the conditions in conjunctive query are sorted according to the frequency/popularity of data fields in the database, which generally reduces the number of decryptions/re-encryptions required for adjustments.

The main idea behind RAEA is to query with conjunction of criteria: 1) sort atomic criteria according to the popularity of fields in a database instance: from low to the high count of fields; 2) proceed gradually with the execution of subqueries by adding one atomic condition at a time; 3) in between make inward adjustments sufficient to proceed with the next subquery; 4) once the execution of the query is completed, make outward adjustments to restore the protection levels.

```
db.collection.find($And:{Name:$eq "Alice", Salary:gt 7000}$)       Q
```

After encrypting the data in the support layers in Q (i.e. $name = $ "$xd37e$" AND $salary = $ "$xe6ue$"), the Inward Adjustment is performed as follows: (i)- The name values in the **whole** database are adjusted to the DET encryption level. (ii)- Salary values found in documents with "$name$" $=$ "$xd37e$" are adjusted to the OPE encryption level. The encrypted query is then performed, and Outward Adjustment is applied in the reverse order of steps ii -> i. In the paper [11], Update-aware adjustment was proposed to decrease communication costs and expose information as well as improve the trade-off between these factors, performance and security in RAEA. Three cases were examined:

- **CASE 1 (Global Update (GU)):** This case involves updating all property values for those documents returned by progressively executing the query, regardless of whether or not they match the current expression. Global Updated data is generated in both the inward and outward adjustment directions.
- **CASE 2 (Necessary Update (NU)):** This case involves updating only property values for those documents returned by progressively executing the query, which refers to those matching the current expression. Necessary Update is also performed in both the inward and outward Encryption adjustment directions.
- **CASE 3 (Zero-Update (ZU)):** It is not necessary to update values in this case. We assume that the documents contain *a unique value property*, whose values serve as *indexes* for the documents. Then Zero-Update policy is accomplished by comparing the current expression to the documents returned. Where matches occur, instead of the property values being updated in the data storage, a copy of the index values of the matching documents is obtained. Zero-Update is also performed in the inward and outward Encryption adjustment directions.

3   Zero Update Encryption Adjustment Case Study

The Zero Update Encryption Adjustment approach is accomplished by performing the query on the encrypted data while utilising adjustment techniques for the data that has been encrypted using Multi-Layer Encryption to achieve the desired result. The primary goal of Zero Update Encryption Adjustment is to prevent the leakage of information to outsourced storage while allowing query capabilities on either the client-side or server-side, depending on the nature of the service providers to outsourced storage. According to the paper [11], Zero Update Encryption Adjustment was tested on OrientDB under only RAEA, which enables for processing queries to be performed on either the client-side or the user-side. The differences in security and performance between the two sides were also discussed in [11]; however, in terms of security, client-side often provides the better protection due to its lack of key exchange. Here, the approach is applied for MongoDB, which does not enable user operations on the server side, thus only client-side will be responsible for processing the query and will not be required to exchange encryption keys with the server side. Two types of adjustment techniques exist on documents database: the Simple Encryption Adjustment (SEA), and Release-Aware Encryption Adjustment (RAEA). The query processing for Zero Update Encryption

Adjustment is accomplished by performing a set of sub-queries to store a list of unique field values of documents that match the expression in the field. In RAEA, for a conjunctive condition, the first sub-query begins with only the first expression and adjusts all values without updating the database, and then stores a list of unique field values of documents that match the first field's expression. The processes are then repeated for the list's subsequent sub-query request documents, which test the current field's expression, update the list, and so on, until the final update of the list matches the query's actual result, as illustrated in an example in Fig. 3.

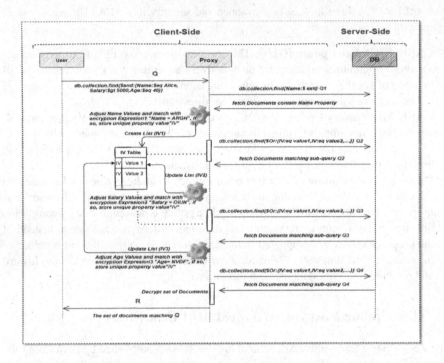

Fig. 3. Zero Update Encryption Adjustment under RAEA Example.

SEA, on the other hand, can reveal more information than requested and slow-down performance due to the number of layers and values adjusted [9,10], however zero-update can also be used in SEA to avoid any information leaking. In SEA, for a conjunctive condition, each sub-query adjusts the fields separately and stores a list of documents with unique field values that match the expression in each field. The end result is the union of all lists of each expression, as shown in example in Fig. 4. Under conjunctive conditions, the security of SEA and RAEA following Zero Update Encryption Adjustment is the same, but RAEA performs better. SEA, on the other hand, can perform any condition, unlike REAE is only conjunctive conditions.

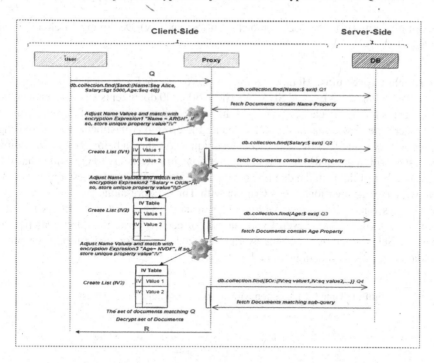

Fig. 4. Zero Update Encryption Adjustment under SEA Example.

4 Zero Update Encryption Adjustment Assessment

Zero Update Encryption Adjustment on the client-side can provide the highest level of security through no revealed information and no exchange keys, but performance must be evaluated more thoroughly; thus, the goal of this section is to study the different scenarios to learn in which one scenario outperforms the other. We concentrate on addressing the following questions:

1. How does the performance of Zero Update Encryption Adjustment under RAEA and SEA affect as the number of expressions in a query grows?
2. How does the performance of Zero Update Encryption Adjustment under RAEA and SEA affect as the number of documents matched by a query grows?
3. How does the usage of cloud providers or indexes impact performance?
4. How does Zero Update Encryption Adjustment perform on MongoDB compare to OrientDB in [11]?
5. Can Zero Update Encryption Adjustment be adapted to work with a different database type?

We provide analytical tests that provide average estimates of execution time for conjunctive conditions via Select, Update and Delete operations.

4.1 Variable Assessment

In this section, questions 1, 2, and 3 are addressed to analyse the effect of variables on performance: (i) The number of criteria expressions; (ii) The number of documents matching result; (iii) The use of index features; and (iv) Deploying to cloud-based storage.

1- Criteria Expressions. Here, we compared Zero Update Encryption Adjustment performance to that of RAEA and SEA. We chose 500,000 documents since we expect the larger size is fetched in cache on the PC which is tested on. The goal of this experiment is to determine how efficient the Zero Update Encryption Adjustment is in increasing expressions or using feasible adjustment techniques. As shown below, Select Operation was tested with a gradually increase of expressions in criteria Q1 to Q7, which has the larger number of fields in the documents: Q1 - Criteria with One Expression; Q2 - Criteria with Two Expressions; Q3 - Criteria with Three Expressions; Q4 - Criteria with Four Expressions; Q5- Criteria with Five Expressions; Q6 - Criteria with Six Expressions; Q7 - Criteria with Seven Expressions. For each criteria, the query was run 30 times for Select operation, and the average was calculated for each of the decryption and data requests, as shown in Table 1.

Table 1. Time for Execution with an increasing number of expressions.

Q	ZU						
	(RAEA)			(SEA)			
	IN-T.	COM-T.	Total	IN-T.	COM-T.	Total	
C1	15226.2	27.2	15253.4	15232.3	23.8	15256.1	
C2	15997.8	30.8	16028.6	30470.2	49	30519.2	
C3	16185.2	32.8	16218	45681.9	84.7	45766.6	
C4	16503.1	36.8	16539.9	60785.3	98.7	60884	
C5	17056.4	41.6	17098	78524.8	125.3	78650.1	
C6	17347.6	45.6	17393.2	91387.8	145.6	91533.4	
C7	17718.1	49.6	17767.7	108726.7	158.9	108885.6	

These findings are summarised in Fig. 5. The findings for the adjustment techniques are significantly different, since the decryption time on SEA doubles as the number of expressions rises. This increase is due to one factor: more SEA values must be decrypted. When compared to SEA, RAEA had increased marginally execution time due to increase number of expressions since there are fewer values to decrypt. While a rise in the number of expressions is effected in the Zero Update Encryption Adjustment under selectivity adjustment techniques which is also a critical factor.

2- Documents Matching Query. One of the goals of this experiment is to evaluate whether or not the number of documents that match a query result has an effect on the

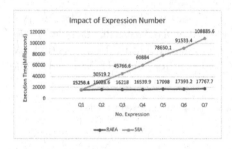

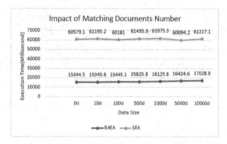

Fig. 5. Analysis Result for increasing the number of expressions.

Fig. 6. Analysis Result for increasing the number of Documents matching Query.

overall performance of the Zero Update Encryption Adjustment under SEA and RAEA. This experiment was carried out on a database that included 500,000 documents. As a result of Experiment above(1), which showed the effect of the number of expressions on performance, the query was performed with a fixed expression. The query has been performed a total of 30 times with increasing the number of document matching. In Table 2, we report the results of experiment 2 in millisecond.

Table 2. Time for Execution with an increasing number of Documents matching Query.

No. Documents Match	ZU					
	(RAEA)			(SEA)		
	IN-T.	COM-T.	Total	IN-T.	COM-T.	Total
0	15321.2	23.3	15344.5	60478.7	100.4	60579.1
10	15322.3	23.5	15345.8	61097.4	97.8	61195.2
100	15421.4	23.7	15445.1	60093.1	87.9	60181
500	15801.3	23.9	15825.8	61345.4	89.9	61435.3
1000	16101.2	24.6	16125.8	61874.1	101.2	61975.3
5000	16402.3	24.4	16424.6	60001.7	92.5	60094.2
10000	17004.6	24.3	17028.9	61120.2	96.9	61217.1
10000	17004.6	24.3	17028.9	61120.2	96.9	61217.1

This experiment (2) demonstrates that increasing the number of documents matching the result has no effect on the SEA adjustment technique, as shown in Fig. 6; nevertheless, increasing the number of documents increases the execution time in the Zero Update Encryption Adjustment in RAEA, but not in SEA.

3- Index Feature. The goal of an index is to speed up search queries by minimizing the number of documents in a collection that could be searched. By default, when a document is generated as an index in MongoDB, the _Id is created. The goal of this experiment is to determine the performance of an index with the Zero Update Encryption Adjustment. The experiment (3) was conducted on a database that included 1,000, 5,000, and 10,000 documents, and the query was conducted using 2 versions (indexed and non-indexed). A total of 30 times were conducted for Select, Update, and Delete operations, as shown in Table 3.

Table 3. Execution Time of Zero-Update using non-indexed vs.indexed

Data Size	Q	Non-Indexed			Indexed		
		IN-T.	COM-T.	Total	IN-T.	COM-T.	Total
1th	Select	31.2	2.9	34.1	31.1	1.4	32.5
	Update	35.7	2.4	38.1	36.8	20.3	57.1
	Delete	30	30.2	60.2	31.4	46.9	78.3
5th	Select	243.9	4.3	248.2	233.1	2.7	235.8
	Update	260.9	4.2	265.1	261.8	46.2	308
	Delete	299.2	73	372.2	286.3	104.6	390.9
10th	Select	323.7	4.6	328.3	322.1	3.3	325.4
	Update	379.4	4.3	383.4	387.7	132.4	520.1
	Delete	369.7	196	565.7	349.7	294.2	643.9

We found that although Select Operations take less time with indexed (see Fig. 7), Update and Delete Operations take more time with indexed (see Figs. 8, and 9). The primary cause for this latency is the cost of re-index computations in the Update and Delete operations, which are not required for the select operation.

4- Cloud. Businesses of various sizes, countries, and industries are increasingly relying on cloud services, which have grown in popularity over the last decade. The goal of this experiment (4) is to evaluate a cloud's performance under the RAEA's Zero Update Encryption Adjustment, which is the effective adjustment technique according to experiment 1 and experiment 2. The experiment was conducted on databases containing 1,000, 5,000, and 10,000 documents, with the query being run using two distinct versions (Local and cloud). Select, Update, and Delete operations were conducted 30 times in total and were taken average execution time as shown in Table 4. While both the Select and Update operations take about the same amount of time for the same number of documents (see Figs. 10, 11), we found that the Delete operation significantly increases cloud time (see Fig. 12). The primary cause of this latency is the expense of the Delete operation's communication.

4.2 Comparing with Different Databases

In this section, questions 4 and 5 are addressed in order to deploy and compare the Zero Update Encryption Adjustment under RAEA, which provides high security and performance on multiple database types (OrientDB and MongoDB) or models (SQL).

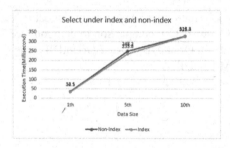 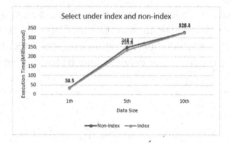

Fig. 7. Execution Time for Select Query using non-indexed vs.indexed.   **Fig. 8.** Execution Time for Update Query using non-indexed vs.indexed.

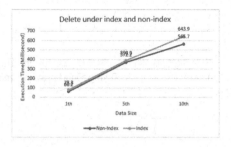

Fig. 9. Execution Time for Delete Query using non-indexed vs.indexed.

1- MongoDB vs OrientDB. Because the approach was previously evaluated on OrientDB, we compared its performance to that of MonogDB, as shown in Table 5. As

Table 4. Execution Time of Zero-Update using cloud provider and Local Storage.

DataSize	Q	Local			cloud		
		IN-T.	COM-T.	Total	IN-T.	COM-T.	Total
1th	Select	31.2	2.9	34.1	37.3	4.8	42.1
	Update	35.7	2.4	38.1	36.8	5.2	42
	Delete	30	30.2	60.2	33.9	413.9	447.8
5th	Select	243.9	4.3	248.2	248.4	8.3	256.7
	Update	260.9	4.2	265.1	266.67	8.2	274.87
	Delete	299.2	73	372.2	279.9	1756	2035.9
10th	Select	323.7	4.6	328.3	334.8	10.1	344.9
	Update	379.4	4.3	383.4	376.4	9.9	386.3
	Delete	369.7	196	565.7	385.9	3486.6	3872.5

a consequence, it seems as if the Select and Update Operations execute effectively on MongoDB than on OrientDB (see Figs. 13 and 14). In comparison to deletion (see Fig. 15), deletion operation executes effectively on OrientDB because OrientDB's connection cost for deletion may be lower than MongoDB's.

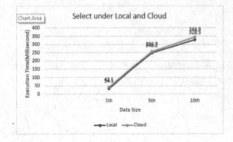

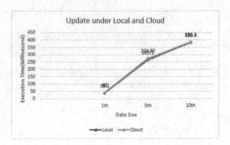

Fig. 10. Execution Time for Select Query using cloud provider and Local Storage.

Fig. 11. Execution Time for Update Query using cloud provider and Local Storage.

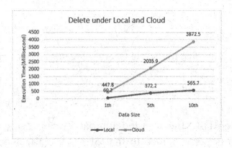

Fig. 12. Execution Time for Delete Query using cloud provider and Local Storage.

Table 5. Execution Time of Zero-Update for OrientDB VS MonogDB.

DataSize	Q	MonogDB			OrientDB		
		IN-T.	COM-T.	Total	IN-T.	COM-T.	Total
1th	Select	31.2	2.9	34.1	34.56	23.56	58.12
	Update	35.7	2.4	38.1	31.19	24.19	55.38
	Delete	30	30.2	60.2	32.19	21.25	53.44
5th	Select	243.9	4.3	248.2	256.19	39.31	295.5
	Update	260.9	4.2	265.1	274.19	43.25	317.44
	Delete	299.2	73	372.2	292.69	40.63	333.32
10th	Select	323.7	4.6	328.3	320.19	54.13	374.32
	Update	379.4	4.3	383.4	387.75	57.75	445.5
	Delete	369.7	196	565.7	335.56	59.69	395.25

2- MongoDB vs MySQL. MongoDB's performance was compared against SQL in a variety of studies, including [2, 15, 18, 21–23, 32], and [27], and MangoDB's performance was shown to be the best. According to our knowledge, the comparison was conducted on unencrypted data only, and therefore the goal here is to verify that MongoDB still outperforms when encryption and adoption of the approach are used as well as an adoption the Zero Update Encryption Adjustment on other database types such as relational databases. As indicated in Table 6, the query was performed on MongoDB and SQL with all affecting variables considered to be constant.

Table 6. Execution Time of Zero-Update for MonogDBVS MySQL.

DataSize	Q	MonogDB			MySQL		
		IN-T.	COM-T.	Total	IN-T.	COM-T.	Total
1th	Select	31.2	2.9	34.1	29.3	45.6	74.9
	Update	35.7	2.4	38.1	37.8	201.4	239.2
	Delete	30	30.2	60.2	31.6	789.1	820.7
5th	Select	243.9	4.3	248.2	257.7	338.6	596.3
	Update	260.9	4.2	265.1	271.6	459.4	731
	Delete	299.2	73	372.2	285.7	1162.2	1447.9
10th	Select	323.7	4.6	328.3	342.3	355.9	698.2
	Update	379.4	4.3	383.4	314.2	1273.5	1587.7
	Delete	369.7	196	565.7	388.9	1601.2	1990.1

As shown in Figs. 16, 17, and 18, MangoDB performs better for all three operations with varying data sizes.

5 Computational Load of Zero Update Encryption Adjustment

As shown via experiments, our approach on MongoDB maximises execution time by offloading the majority of the computational load from data owners and query users to the client-side (proxy). Additionally, the majority of time is spent on adjustment processing, which is expected for multi-layers encryption. The goal of this section is to assess the effects of multi-layer on computational load on our approach from the perspective of data owners and query users. To begin, data owners encrypt data using multiple layers; as a result, we compare data encrypted time using multiple layers to data encrypted using a single layer (see Table 7).

Table 7. Encryption cost using Single layer VS Multi-layers.

Data Size	Muti-layer Encryption	One-Layer Encryption
	Encryption Time	Encryption Time
1thu	1319.4	201.4
5thu	3739.1	392.3
10thu	6788.2	707.2

Figure 19 illustrates how multi-layer technology raises the computational load on data owners.

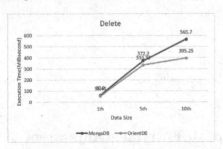

Fig. 13. Execution Time for Select Query using MongoDB and OrientDB.

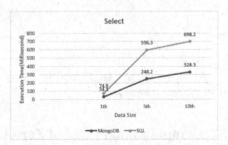

Fig. 14. Execution Time for Update Query using MongoDB and OrientDB.

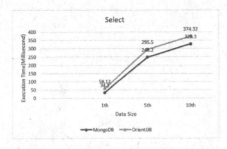

Fig. 15. Execution Time for Delete Query using MongoDB and OrientDB.

Fig. 16. Execution Time for Select Query using MongoDB and MySQL.

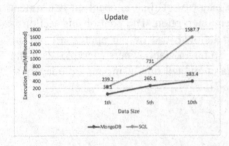

Fig. 17. Execution Time for Update Query using MongoDB and MySQL.

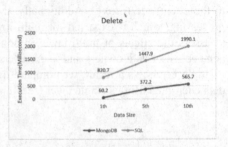

Fig. 18. Execution Time for Delete Query using MongoDB and MySQL.

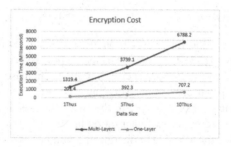

Fig. 19. Analysis Encryption cost using Single layer VS Multi-layers.

Second, the proxy carries the computational load associated with a user query to adjust layers; therefore, to assess this and compare it to multi-layer adjustment as shown in Table 8, we assumed that data owners encrypted data using a single layer and also applied Zero Update Encryption Adjustment as follows: proxy adjusts the layer to plaintext and compares it to the expression constant, rather than adjusting the layers to encryption support and comparing it to the encryption constant.

Table 8. Experiment Result of executing query on Single layer Vs. multi-layers.

DataSize	Q	Mulit-layers			Single-layer		
		IN-T.	COM-T.	Total	IN-T.	COM-T.	Total
1th	Select	31.2	2.9	34.1	18.4	2.1	20.5
	Update	35.7	2.4	38.1	20.4	2.6	23
	Delete	30	30.2	60.2	17.6	29.7	47.3
5th	Select	243.9	4.3	248.2	90.2	3.6	93.8
	Update	260.9	4.2	265.1	91.8	3.8	95.6
	Delete	299.2	73	372.2	93.6	69.6	163.2
10th	Select	323.7	4.6	328.3	192.96	4.3	197.26
	Update	379.4	4.3	383.4	197	4.4	201.4
	Delete	369.7	196	565.7	198.8	184.8	383.6

Figures 20, 21, and 22 illustrate these compute demands resulting from multi-layer and single-layer user queries for all three operations;the high cost involved in adjustment was due to multi-layer.

6   Performance and Security Analysis

This section provides a detailed analysis of the outcome performance and security while using the Zero Update Encryption Adjustment.

6.1 Performance Analysis

The adjustment requires the most execution time when it comes to generating an encrypted database from the Data Owner or adjusting processing based on a user query. The reason for this is that multi-layer encryption due to increase encryption cost from data owner and decryption cost from user query but this cost is within reasonable limits. To minimise the cost of encryption, the two solutions to minimise decryption costs is either to lower the number of encryption layers or lower the number of values decryption. As a result, the variables affecting the number of these values and therefore Zero Update Encryption Adjustment must be assessed using the proper adjustment techniques, which are SEA and RAEA for the Document-Database based on [11].

Even though SEA decrypts all field values, these values increase as the number of fields (i.e. Expressions) in the query increases; thus, the number of fields is a significant variable; whereas, RAEA gradually determines the values based on its matching of a subset of the result; thus, here, the number of documents matching the result is a significant variable. As a result, it is essential to measure the impact of these two variables on ZU when using various adjudication techniques. Experiments demonstrate the following effects of two factors on Zero Update Encryption Adjustment:

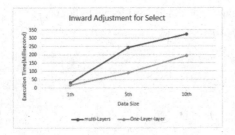

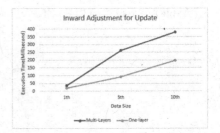

Fig. 20. Execution Time for Select Query using Multi-layers and Single-layer.

Fig. 21. Execution Time for Update Query using Multi-layers and Single-layer.

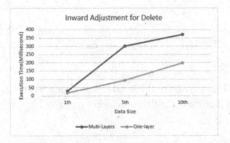

Fig. 22. Execution Time for Delete Query using Multi-layers and Single-layer.

1. The number of expressions or fields in the query: this has a significant impact on SEA, but has little effect on RAEA.
2. Number of matching documents: this has no impact on SEA, but has a significant effect on RAEA.

Regardless of the impact of matching documents on RAEA, it remains more effective than SEA until all documents in the collection match the query, at which point it performs as well as SEA, which is a rare situation.

However, the feature of this technique is that the procedure may be performed through the index. Additionally, ZU outperforms the competition in terms of search indexing. As a result, the index imposes the minimal computational load on the client. Finally, ZU requires the most amount of time to execute throughout the adjustment process. However, based on the outcomes of the experiment, this additional overhead is within reasonable limits.

Since MongoDB involves use of indexes, ZU has to be tested against them; we get the following result experiment:

– Zero Update Encryption Adjustment under index speeds the Select operation and delays the Update and Delete operations as with plaintext data.

ZeroDB uses a B-Tree index, which needs several rounds of connection with the base to execute each expression, while Zero Update Encryption Adjustment requires just one round, resulting in a significant communication cost for ZeroDB. Thus, ZU's index-based approach is still more effective than ZeroDB.

6.2 Security Analysis

The server never sees the plaintext in [4, 5, 9, 34], but it may disclose some information about the data, such as equal values or the order in which the update layer is adjusted; the leak issue was addressed by the Zero Update Encryption Adjustment. The Zero Update Encryption Adjustment enabled the adjustment to be made without requiring any updates, and all data remained in the most secure layer that does not leak any information. However, if the Zero Update Encryption Adjustment is used on the server-side, as this option does in OrientDB [10], the encryption keys for all requested levels except the latter inner layer must be provided to the server. This may result in key abuse in the case of an honest but curious database management system (DBMS) or an external attack. MongoDB addresses this issue by eliminating server-side decryption or adjustment in the case of a zero-update and switching the load to the client (Proxy and User Application). This requires the client to supply a proxy with strict security requirements, and in the case of an attack, the keys may be used against current users, with the potential of explicit data exposure owing to the availability of keys for the latter inner layer. As a result, we will assume that the proxy is trusted in this case. For example, if the proxy is semi-trusted, it is possible to prohibit the proxy from having access to the keys in the latter inner layer and to make the user application responsible for decryption this layer.

7 Experiments with Large Scale Dataset

In this section we use Yelp [1], a big real-world dataset, to assesses the efficiency and scalability of the zero update's novel result, Zero update adjustment under RAEA. Yelp has 7 million business reviews, and each reviewer document has seven fields: review ID, business ID, user ID, stars, helpful, funny, and cool. Three queries were used on this dataset to assess the connection time (con.) and adjustment time (adj.) using select, update, and delete for conjunction conditions in the selection predicates. Our tests were performed on a Windows 10 PC with an Intel Core 5, 1.80 GHz CPU, 16 GB RAM, and a 1 TB hard drive. All recorded timings were millisecond averaged over 30 runs. This is illustrated in Table 9, which compares plaintext processing against Zero update adjustment.

Figure 23 shows the total execution time of zero update adjustment processing query, as well as the plaintext. Adjustments layers and the cost of connection mean zero update adjustment requires more time. However, it still offers confidentiality.

Table 9. Query processing time for the plaintext vs zero update.

	Plaintext			Zero-update		
	IN-T.	COM-T.	Total	IN-T.	COM-T.	Total
Select	-	3.8	3.8	75406	8956.4	84362.47
Update	-	4.8	4.8	76247.8	4420.8	80668.6
Delete	-	1626.8	1626.8	75824.6	4454.2	80278.8

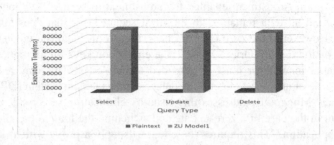

Fig. 23. Comparing the total execution time for Plaintext vs. Zero update of query processing.

There are two possible ways to shorten the execution time. The first involves using a proxy with high specifications and resources where connection and adjustment take place, as in Hacigumus et al. [26] and Monomi [37]. However, modern data storage environments mean such high-specification proxies would be expensive. The proxy must be small and use the minimum possible processing resources and storage space [35]. As a consequence, the data owner could choose to process the data on an internal server rather than an external server if the proxy was too big and expensive. The second option would be to decrease the number of layers and connection round times. This would minimize connection and adjustment costs while also achieving scalability, which is one of our research goals. Due to the minimal amounts of data in all of our previous experiments, we slightly modified our policy to greatly reduce on the connection rounds. Algorithms 1 and 2 note that model 1 needs an equal number of rounds for each property, whereas model 2 only requires one round as plaintext. In Model 2, this is accomplished by checking the gradual matching of expressions at the same time and storing only a list of document indexes that match all expressions. In Model 1, each expression is checked and a list of document indexes that match it is stored and used in the subsequent expression, which calls for a new connection round, and so forth.

Data: $Criteria \leftarrow e_1, e_2, \ldots e_n$
Result: $U \leftarrow$ unique list values matching query criteria;
$n \leftarrow$ the number of properties containing criteria ;
$N_u \leftarrow$ the number of documents containing values in a unique list;
$N_p \leftarrow$ the number of documents containing property;
while $N_p \neq 0$ do
  ;   /* this is communication round */
  if $property(e1)$ *value matches* e_1 then
    | $U \leftarrow$ index of document;
  end
end
while $N_U \neq 0$ do
  ;   /* this is communication round */
  if $property(e2)$ *value matches* e_2 then
    | $U \leftarrow$ index of document;
  end
end
....
while $N_U \neq 0$ do
  ;   /* this is communication round */
  if $property(en)$ *value matches* e_n then
    | $U \leftarrow$ index of document;
  end
end

Algorithm 1. Model 1(Scenario A).

Data: $Criteria \leftarrow e_1, e_2, \ldots e_n$
Result: $U \leftarrow$ unique list values matching query criteria;
$n \leftarrow$ the number of properties containing criteria;
$N_u \leftarrow$ the number of documents containing values in a unique list;
$N_p \leftarrow$ the number of documents containing property;
while $N_p \neq 0$ do
  ;   /* this is communication round */
  if $property(e1)$ *value matches* e_1 then
    if $property(e2)$ *value matches* e_2 then
      .... if $property(en)$ *value matches* e_n
      then
      | $U \leftarrow$ index of document;
    end
  end
end

Algorithm 2. Model 2(Scenario B.)

The query execution time for modification zero update to plaintext and previous Zero-update was compared, as outlined in Table 10. Figure 24 shows that the modified Zero update, model 2, takes less time to process queries than the original Zero update, model 1. As can be seen in Fig. 25, the communication time for model 2 is almost identical to the communication time for plaintext.

Table 10. Query processing time for the plaintext vs Zero update models.

	Plaintext			Zero-update Model 1(Scenario A)			Zero-update model 2(Scenario B)		
	IN-T.	COM-T.	Total	IN-T.	COM-T.	Total	IN-T.	COM-T.	Total
Select	-	3.8	3.8	75406	8956.4	84362.4	74576.2	3.6	74579.8
Update	-	4.8	4.8	76247.8	4420.8	80668.6	74675	19.8	74694.8
Delete	-	1626.8	1626.8	75824.6	4454.2	80278.8	74153.2	2458.4	76611.6

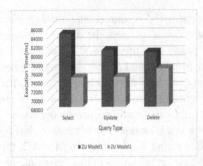 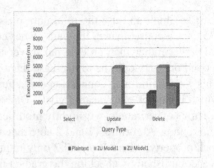

Fig. 24. Comparing the total execution time for Zero update of model 1 vs. model 2 of query processing.   **Fig. 25.** Communication time for the plaintext vs Zero update models.

8   Related Work

There are efforts and research studies devoted to querying encrypted data, which may be classified as hardware-based approaches (e.g., [12, 14]) or software-based approaches (e.g., [6–8, 24, 26, 28, 31, 33–35, 37, 39, 40]). There are numerous examples of the software approach assigning overload computation to either the client or the server or dividing it between the two. This approach contrasts with ZeroDB [29], which performs all overload computation on the client-side. In [26, 28, 31, 33, 35, 37, 40], one of the [13, 17, 20, 25, 30, 36] algorithms encrypts data and query over encrypted data, enabling a particular type of computation with a varying degree of data leakage. While [6, 34, 39] can encrypt data through multi-layer derived from these algorithms, they require adjustment techniques that enable more classes of computation. [3, 9–11, 34] have suggested adjustment techniques that offer a certain amount of exposing information to the database; however, the Zero Update Encryption Adjustment prevents any such leakages from occurring.

9   Summary

In this paper, we examine the Zero Update Encryption Adjustment on MonogDB, which enables queries over encrypted data with multiple layers of encryption without disclosing any information to the DBMS and no exchange keys. We investigate the variables that affect performance, namely the amount of expressions and the matching result. The suggested approach is implemented in an OrientDB and SQL environment. The results of our experiments show that ZU is effective when used to a large-scale encrypted dataset and conjunctive condition query. Other conditions, such as not being supported by RAEA by SEA, can be performed, but at the sacrifice of performance to security. Any previous kind of adjustment or RAEA could maintain their performance level while ensuring maximum security in terms of data leakage. The Zero Update Encryption Adjustment can be used with any SQL or NoSQL database. As part of the future work, decreasing the adjustment time will be optimised RAEA or SEA efficiency. Future work will attempt to optimise efficiency by decreasing the adjustment time.

References

1. yelp dataset. https://www.yelp.com/dataset. Accessed 2 July 2022
2. Aboutorabi, S.H., Rezapour, M., Moradi, M., Ghadiri, N.: Performance evaluation of SQL and MongoDB databases for big e-commerce data. In: 2015 International Symposium on Computer Science and Software Engineering (CSSE), pp. 1–7. IEEE (2015)
3. Aburawi, N., Coenen, F., Lisitsa, A.: Traversal-aware encryption adjustment for graph databases
4. Aburawi, N., Coenen, F., Lisitsa, A.: Traversal-aware encryption adjustment for graph databases. In: DATA, pp. 381–387 (2018)
5. Aburawi, N., Coenen, F., Lisitsa, A.: Querying encrypted data in graph databases. In: Khalaf, M.I., Al-Jumeily, D., Lisitsa, A. (eds.) ACRIT 2019. CCIS, vol. 1174, pp. 367–382. Springer, Cham (2020). https://doi.org/10.1007/978-3-030-38752-5_29
6. Aburawi, N., Lisitsa, A., Coenen, F.: Querying encrypted graph databases. In: Proceedings of the 4th International Conference on Information Systems Security and Privacy. SCITEPRESS-Science and Technology Publications (2018)
7. Almarwani, M., Konev, B., Lisitsa, A.: Fine-grained access control for querying over encrypted document-oriented database. In: Mori, P., Furnell, S., Camp, O. (eds.) ICISSP 2019. CCIS, vol. 1221, pp. 403–425. Springer, Cham (2020). https://doi.org/10.1007/978-3-030-49443-8_19
8. Almarwani, M., Konev, B., Lisitsa, A.: Flexible access control and confidentiality over encrypted data for document-based database. In: Proceedings of the 4th International Conference on Information Systems Security and Privacy. SCITEPRESS-Science and Technology Publications (2019)
9. Almarwani, M., Konev, B., Lisitsa, A.: Release-aware encryption adjustment query processing for document database. In: Proceedings of the 4th International Conference on Information Systems Security and Privacy. SCITEPRESS-Science and Technology Publications (2020)
10. Almarwani, M., Konev, B., Lisitsa, A.: Release-aware in-out encryption adjustment in MongoDB query processing. In: Proceedings of the 4th International Conference on Information Systems Security and Privacy. SCITEPRESS-Science and Technology Publications (2021)
11. Almarwani, M., Konev, B., Lisitsa, A.: Efficient and secure encryption adjustment for JSON data. In: Proceedings of the 4th International Conference on Information Systems Security and Privacy. SCITEPRESS-Science and Technology Publications (2022)
12. Arasu, A., et al.: Orthogonal security with cipherbase. In: CIDR (2013)
13. Arasu, A., Eguro, K., Kaushik, R., Ramamurthy, R.: Querying encrypted data (tutorial). In: 2014 ACM SIGMOD Conference, June 2014. https://www.microsoft.com/en-us/research/publication/querying-encrypted-data-tutorial-2/
14. Bajaj, S., Sion, R.: TrustedDB: a trusted hardware-based database with privacy and data confidentiality. IEEE Trans. Knowl. Data Eng. **26**(3), 752–765 (2013)
15. Bharti, S.: Security analysis of MongoDB and its comparison with relational databases
16. Boldyreva, A., Chenette, N., Lee, Y., O'Neill, A.: Order-preserving symmetric encryption. In: Joux, A. (ed.) EUROCRYPT 2009. LNCS, vol. 5479, pp. 224–241. Springer, Heidelberg (2009). https://doi.org/10.1007/978-3-642-01001-9_13
17. Boldyreva, A., Chenette, N., O'Neill, A.: Order-preserving encryption revisited: improved security analysis and alternative solutions. In: Rogaway, P. (ed.) CRYPTO 2011. LNCS, vol. 6841, pp. 578–595. Springer, Heidelberg (2011). https://doi.org/10.1007/978-3-642-22792-9_33
18. Čerešňák, R., Kvet, M.: Comparison of query performance in relational a non-relation databases. Transp. Res. Procedia **40**, 170–177 (2019)

19. OrientDB community: OrientDB documentation (2022). https://orientdb.org/. Accessed 1 July 2022
20. Daemen, J., Rijmen, V.: AES proposal: Rijndael (1999)
21. Chang, M.-L.E., Chua, H.N.: SQL and NoSQL database comparison. In: Arai, K., Kapoor, S., Bhatia, R. (eds.) FICC 2018. AISC, vol. 886, pp. 294–310. Springer, Cham (2019). https://doi.org/10.1007/978-3-030-03402-3_20
22. Deari, R., Zenuni, X., Ajdari, J., Ismaili, F., Raufi, B.: Analysis and comparison of document-based databases with SQL relational databases: MongoDB vs MySQL. In: Proceedings of the International Conference on Information Technologies (InfoTech 2018), pp. 1–10 (2018)
23. Dipina Damodaran, B., Salim, S., Vargese, S.M.: Performance evaluation of MySQL and MongoDB databases. Int. J. Cybern. Inform. (IJCI) 5 (2016)
24. Egorov, M., Wilkison, M.: Zerodb White paper. arXiv preprint arXiv:1602.07168 (2016)
25. ElGamal, T.: A public key cryptosystem and a signature scheme based on discrete logarithms. IEEE Trans. Inf. Theory 31(4), 469–472 (1985)
26. Hacigümüş, H., Iyer, B., Li, C., Mehrotra, S.: Executing SQL over encrypted data in the database-service-provider model. In: Proceedings of the 2002 ACM SIGMOD International Conference on Management of Data, pp. 216–227 (2002)
27. Keshavarz, S.: Analyzing performance differences between MySQL and MongoDB (2021)
28. Li, J., Liu, Z., Chen, X., Xhafa, F., Tan, X., Wong, D.S.: L-encdb: a lightweight framework for privacy-preserving data queries in cloud computing. Knowl.-Based Syst. 79, 18–26 (2015)
29. Mitterer, M., Niedermayer, H., von Maltitz, M., Carle, G.: An experimental performance analysis of the cryptographic database ZeroDB. In: Proceedings of the 1st Workshop on Privacy by Design in Distributed Systems, pp. 1–5 (2018)
30. Paillier, P.: Public-key cryptosystems based on composite degree residuosity classes. In: Stern, J. (ed.) EUROCRYPT 1999. LNCS, vol. 1592, pp. 223–238. Springer, Heidelberg (1999). https://doi.org/10.1007/3-540-48910-X_16
31. Pappas, V., et al.: Blind seer: a scalable private DBMS. In: 2014 IEEE Symposium on Security and Privacy, pp. 359–374. IEEE (2014)
32. Patel, S., Kumar, S., Katiyar, S., Shanmugam, R., Chaudhary, R.: MongoDB vs MySQL: a comparative study of MongoDB and MySQL based on their performance. Technical report, EasyChair (2020)
33. Poddar, R., Boelter, T., Popa, R.A.: ARX: a strongly encrypted database system. IACR Cryptol. ePrint Arch. 2016, 591 (2016)
34. Popa, R.A., Redfield, C., Zeldovich, N., Balakrishnan, H.: CryptDB: protecting confidentiality with encrypted query processing. In: Proceedings of the Twenty-Third ACM Symposium on Operating Systems Principles, pp. 85–100. ACM (2011)
35. Sarfraz, M.I., Nabeel, M., Cao, J., Bertino, E.: DBmask: fine-grained access control on encrypted relational databases. In: Proceedings of the 5th ACM Conference on Data and Application Security and Privacy, pp. 1–11. ACM (2015)
36. Song, D.X., Wagner, D., Perrig, A.: Practical techniques for searches on encrypted data. In: Proceeding 2000 IEEE Symposium on Security and Privacy. S&P 2000, pp. 44–55. IEEE (2000)
37. Tu, S.L., Kaashoek, M.F., Madden, S.R., Zeldovich, N.: Processing analytical queries over encrypted data (2013)
38. Tutorialspoint: MongoDB-java, November 2020. https://db-engines.com/en/ranking. Accessed 20 Nov 2020

39. Waage, T., Wiese, L.: Property preserving encryption in NoSQL wide column stores. In: Panetto, H., et al. (eds.) OTM 2017. LNCS, vol. 10574, pp. 3–21. Springer, Cham (2017). https://doi.org/10.1007/978-3-319-69459-7_1
40. Xu, G., Ren, Y., Li, H., Liu, D., Dai, Y., Yang, K.: CryptMDB: a practical encrypted MongoDB over big data. In: 2017 IEEE International Conference on Communications (ICC), pp. 1–6. IEEE (2017)

Evaluating Consumer Understanding and Awareness of Connected and Autonomous Vehicle Data Privacy

Flora Barber[1]([⊠]) [iD] and Steven Furnell[2] [iD]

[1] WMG, University of Warwick, Coventry, UK
Flora.Barber@warwick.ac.uk
[2] School of Computer Science, University of Nottingham, Nottingham, UK
Steven.Furnell@nottingham.ac.uk

Abstract. Connected and Autonomous Vehicles (CAVs) are significantly transforming the definition 'vehicle' on the road and in the market through their disruptive and pervasive technologies. Stakeholder research has consistently overlooked consumers and their CAV privacy knowledge. This paper addresses this through evaluating the consumer's current privacy knowledge through a survey, focus group, and analysis of manufacturer's privacy provisions. It found the materials insufficient, leaving consumers unsure of their vehicle's data collecting functionalities. In this study, 168 survey respondents and 6 focus group participants were consulted, and their responses studied using thematic analysis. The results highlight the consumer's need to be 'Informed', particularly in relation to themes around the requirements and provision of information, as well as the communication and control of privacy. Further themes such as 'Disinterest' and 'Distrust' emerged from the focus group. This paper recommends industry prioritisation of consumer education, introducing vehicle-specific data protection legislation, government assurance of manufacturer compliance, and use of the manufacturer's app to control privacy. Vehicle purchasers must be informed of a vehicle's data transmission, collection, and protection technologies, and how to make use of its privacy controls.

Keywords: Connected and autonomous vehicles · Consumer behaviour · User acceptance · Privacy awareness

1 Introduction

It is forecast that the gigabyte of data collected by Connected and Autonomous Vehicles (CAVs) per second [2] will be worth $750 billion in monetisation by 2030 [3]. As connectivity and autonomy are newer additions to vehicular functionality, researchers have raised concerns that security has become an afterthought [4, 5]. Data can be leaked to a threat actor remotely and locally, impacting both multiple and specific vehicles [6]. It is reported that 45% of new buyers express concern about the detriment these new technologies may have on their privacy [7]. Consumers already face challenges understanding the privacy options available on the devices they currently use. It is, therefore, vital to take a consumer-centric approach in consulting the end-users as stakeholders to ascertain their knowledge and improve public's confidence in CAVs. Vehicle users must be able to make informed privacy decisions if CAV deployment is to be a success. This paper addresses these gaps by creating a consumer data and privacy knowledge benchmark through consumer consultation.

This paper defines CAVs as vehicles with some level of capacity to "understand its surroundings, move, navigate and behave responsibly without human input, and at the same time has connectivity functions enabling it to be proactive, cooperative, well-informed and coordinated" [8]. However, the consumer's perception of what a vehicle is and does is not aligned with the vehicles on today's market, where the pace of innovation has transformed the once isolated vehicles into CAVs. Therefore, this discussion focuses on assessing consumer awareness and understanding of their own vehicle's data collecting components and manufacturer's privacy materials, and how they believe their engagement with vehicular privacy would be increased. This paper finds that current manufacturer privacy materials insufficiently engage consumers with their vehicular privacy, particularly when detailing to users how their data is collected and used. Focus group participants suggested a variety of approaches to improve consumer engagement and trust. This paper contributes to the wider documented understanding of consumer's CAV knowledge by specifically consulting consumers about their data privacy knowledge both widely through surveys and in depth through a focus group. The findings compliment those from interviews with CAV experts about cyber security and privacy in CAVs [9], and the more generalised study by Maeng et al. [10] into consumers' attitudes towards CAV-related information security threats.

This paper is an extended and revised version of "Benchmarking Consumer Data and Privacy Knowledge in Connected and Autonomous Vehicles" [1] presented at the 8th International Conference on Information Systems Security and Privacy (ICISSP) 2022. The structure, recruitment, limitations, and execution of the survey and focus group are detailed in depth alongside the analysis process used. Each theme and sub-theme have been given individual extended sections, complemented with participants' quotes. The related work section has been subdivided and enriched with additional studies. Conclusions have been expanded upon with acknowledgement of the paper's achievements, limitations, and future research opportunities.

The paper begins with a review of all the current literature and research into CAVs and consumer data and privacy knowledge. The remainder is formed of two parts: Sect. 3 benchmarks the information that is currently available to the consumer through the analysis of the privacy information provided by six vehicle manufacturers in their vehicle handbook, in-vehicle infotainment system, and on their respective websites. The results of this analysis will be used to understand the extent and content of privacy knowledge that is clearly declared in the consumer domain. The consultation of the consumer as a stakeholder is covered in the research methodology in Sect. 4 and results in Sect. 5. The consumer's level of knowledge is identified through an anonymous survey with results of interest followed up with a small virtual focus group where participant responses will be used to inform and direct the discussion. Section 6 concludes the paper with an evaluation of the study's limitations, recommendations, and potential avenues for future research.

2 Related Work

This section demonstrates the current gaps in the research area's literature through the analysis of related work, subdivided into four areas of interest: The importance of vehicular data privacy, the education of the consumer, obtaining consumer trust, and consulting the consumer in research.

2.1 The Importance of Vehicular Data Privacy

It has been determined that drivers can be fingerprinted with 100% accuracy solely on 8 min of brake pedal data [11], purely acceleration data [12], a combination of sensors [13], or mapping the location of journeys without GPS either through fog nodes data near the vehicle's journey [14] or from vehicle speed, waiting at traffic lights, and turns [15]. This reveals that users, unaware of this range and number of uniquely identifying parameters, can be individually identified by data that is not classed as personal under current GDPR regulations. In light of the Facebook-Cambridge Analytica data scandal and the multimillion fines against technology corporations for breaching data protection rules [16], consumers are wary of their data's security, from it being sold to third parties to turning the relatively anonymous and private space of a vehicle into a means of surveillance to profile and predict their behaviour [17, 18]. None of the vehicles in one study were found to be compliant with any current data privacy legislation, and the sharing or re-use of their data was not transparent [19].

Current automotive manufacturer privacy policies have been found to be lengthy and confusing with their use of legal and technical terms and fail to define the "legitimate business purposes" used as a reason for collecting data [20]. This gives consumers few real insights and options to control the data collected about them without reducing vehicle functionality. Tesla's telematics policy notes that opting out could cause damage to the vehicle or reduce serviceability [21], leaving the consumer with no choice but to accept their policies if they are to drive the vehicle [18]. Users may face insurance complications for not keeping their vehicle up to date in the event of an accident, especially if the manufacturer claims that it might have been avoided if the user had opted into the policy. This lack of choice diminishes the positive impacts to personal autonomy that CAVs have, especially for those unable to drive themselves, as it brings a cost or trading element to the anticipated freedoms of self-determined mobility access [18]. Further research has found that no original equipment manufacturer (OEM) details the data it is collecting, who has access to or uses it, the security in place to protect it, or that real time querying may occur unknown to the consumer, despite researchers discovering that this data could be accessed via the vehicle's VIN at a car dealer [22]. This secrecy and obscurity within the industry has been previously abused by manufacturers such as in the Volkswagen emissions scandal, which has likewise damaged consumer trust [22].

2.2   The Education of the Consumer

The importance of CAV consumer training has been identified, but not prioritised, by the United Nations Economic and Social Council (ECOSOC) World Forum for Harmonization of Vehicle Regulations [23]. The Society of Motor Manufacturers and Traders has called on the UK Government to provide consumers with a singular clear educational resource designed for potential buyers, aiming to increase public confidence in the automotive industry, its data privacy, and the safety provisions and protections of CAVs [24]. This consumer campaign has yet to be realised, but previous attempts include a consumer guide on personal data in CAVs. This guide offered two websites created for consumer education, one explaining new safety features and terms (mycardoeswhat.org) and another specialising in CAV data privacy (automotiveprivacy.com) [25]. However, the former site is full of broken links and the latter is no longer available, leaving consumers again without resources. Currently the front line of consumer education and support rests with car dealerships, yet their purpose to market and sell their products adds possible bias to the information they may provide [26]. An independent and impartial investigation branch, like those for both air and rail accidents, is proposed in one study, which would be beneficial in managing liability and increasing public confidence by conducting investigations transparently [26].

2.3   Obtaining Consumer Trust

Consumer trust, readiness, and acceptability is one of ten priority areas that has been identified by researchers as imperative to the success of CAVs [8]. Consumers are at risk of their data being targeted by hackers for purposes of extortion, increasing the credibility of targeted social engineering attacks, burglary, and exploitation as a back door into companies for intellectual property or data theft [27]. Consumers have expressed concern about insurers tracking them and this data being sold on to third parties without their consent or knowledge [15]. Data protections must not endanger the low latency connectivity that is vital for CAV safety critical systems, and be transparent about such choices with the consumer, where it is safe to do so [6, 28].

As the average vehicle life span is 13.9 years, a figure exceeding that of many operating systems, new vehicular security systems must be flexible to change and work consistently to protect user data [29]. Researchers propose vehicle specific solutions such as a Differentially Private Data Streaming (DPDS) system to address privacy weakness in distributed edge computing, guaranteeing privacy levels over time and when vehicles dynamically move over time [30], a start, predict, mitigate, and test (SPMT) system to predict and mitigate vulnerabilities systematically [5], and an architecture (CARAMEL) that detects attacks, provides in-vehicle anti-hacking measures, and real time validation of vehicle data transmissions integrity [31]. Such solutions are part of several tools that need to be considered. It is crucial that regulation is brought up to date to reassure consumers and demonstrate respect for user privacy, ensuring that CAV users have control over all aspects of their data [4, 17].

2.4 Consulting the Consumer in Research

Whilst stakeholders such as insurers and manufacturers have been consulted and incorporated into the UK Government's initiatives to strengthen the cybersecurity aspects of CAVs, the consumer has been regularly omitted from formal consultation [32]. The proposed assurance framework for assessing a CAV's cyber security level, known as the 5StarS initiative, is designed to support consumers and insurers in understanding the cyber security risk of vehicles independently tested under the framework [32]. It follows on from the industry and consumer success of Euro NCAP's 5-star rating assurance framework for the safety of passenger vehicles. Whilst the 5StarS initiative seeks to increase consumer confidence through ensuring all parts of a CAV's conception and life cycle is cyber secure, the consumer was not consulted in the research [32]. The insurer is given a more detailed score breakdown for purposes of calculating group ratings, but despite this impacting consumer's insurance premiums the insurer's score is not made public. The consumer is, therefore, unable to see which principles the CAV they are purchasing is strong or weak in, with the vehicle's notes for Category 7 of the Principles (which concerns data transmission and storage), being publicly unavailable [32]. The Euro NCAP scheme, in contrast, makes all test results visible with written sub-section notes alongside its star rating.

3 Data Privacy Materials Available to the Consumer

This section examines the data privacy information publicly available to the consumer in their owner's manual, via the in-vehicle infotainment system, and in the manufacturer's privacy policy provided on their respective website. The findings are summarised in Table 1. As not all vehicle manufacturers have dedicated mobile applications, the privacy information supplied by such apps has not been included. It is vital to understand the resources currently available to consumers to contextualise their knowledge. For this evaluation six manufacturers (Audi (Volkswagen Group), BMW (BMW AG), Ford, Tesla, Toyota (Toyota (GB) Plc.), and Volvo (Geely)) were selected to embody a range of modern vehicles currently in production and were chosen from the top 15 'Most innovative Automotive OEMs of 2021', as ranked by the Center of Automotive Management [33], and from the top 15 manufacturers by market capitalisation [34]. Characteristics of the vehicles chosen are presented in Table 2. The owner's manuals and privacy policies were evaluated from a consumer's perspective for their ease of use when locating privacy information. All documentation was manually evaluated using document analysis by one researcher.

The parameters are grouped into the three main outlets of privacy information that vehicle manufacturers provide: the in-vehicle infotainment system, the vehicle handbook/owner's manual, and the manufacturer's website. The parameters for the infotainment system (such as determining if the data transmission settings could be adjusted and the software release notes viewed) were answered using the vehicle handbooks. The ability to access a copy of the handbook via the infotainment system was determined to establish alternative ways consumers can conveniently retrieve privacy information. The manufacturer's websites were checked for software notes as these are an important method of engaging consumers with their vehicular data privacy by understanding the functions and abilities their vehicle possesses and the protections in place. The manufacturer's websites were judged for their signposting to and ease of navigating through their privacy policy, which when unclear or convoluted may dissuade consumers from engaging with privacy information and weaken their privacy knowledge. The vehicle handbooks were analysed for clearly signposted information about vehicular privacy, the use of dedicated privacy chapters, Event Data Recorders, and how to update the vehicle, including references to full copies of the manufacturer's privacy policy. It is imperative that this information, and all other data collecting and recording features of the vehicle, are clearly explained to the consumer for transparency and trust. Vehicle software updates are vital in maintaining the cyber security protections of the vehicle, thus protecting the consumer's privacy and data. The websites and owner's manuals were also analysed for material that emphasised the importance of and methods to remove personal data from a vehicle before sale.

Table 1. Summary of privacy information available to consumers from selected manufacturers [1]. Key: Y = Yes, N = No, P = Partially available depending on regions/vehicle/manufacturer.

Criteria		Manufacturer					
		Audi	BMW	Ford	Tesla	Toyota	Volvo
In-vehicle	Access to copy of owner's manual?	N	Y	N	Y	N	Y
	Access privacy information and settings?	Y	P	Y	Y	N	Y
	Software release notes available	P	N	N	Y	N	Y
Owner's manual	Privacy information included	Y	P	Y	Y	P	Y
	Dedicated chapter on data protection	Y	N	Y	N	N	Y
	Notes where to find privacy policy	Y	N	Y	Y	N	Y
	Event Data Recorder information	Y	Y	Y	P	P	Y
	Remove in-vehicle personal data?	N	Y	Y	Y	N	Y
	Information on how to update vehicle	Y	N	Y	Y	N	Y
	Clear who should update vehicle	N	N	N	Y	N	N
Website	Ease of privacy policy navigation	N	Y	N	Y	Y	Y
	Emphasis on personal data removal	N	N	Y	N	Y	N
	Software release notes available	N	Y	N	N	N	Y

Using document analysis, Audi's privacy information was found to be generally well written, yet their privacy policy was very difficult to locate and had conflicting advice on who is responsible for vehicular updates. Ford offered impressive online provisions through a policy 'hub' and its manual contained a thorough and detailed 'Data Privacy' chapter. However, its density could be better managed by using subdivided sections and hyperlinked buttons as BMW used, making its online materials much easier to navigate. Yet, BMW's vehicle handbook failed to mention any privacy information despite having 'ConnectedDrive' features. In contrast, Volvo's materials were very comprehensive throughout and included a software release notes finder. Only Tesla specified who is responsible for software updates, but its owner's manual lacked a dedicated privacy section. Toyota's manual provided the least amount of privacy information of those compared, but their website, like Audi's handbook, placed significant focus on deleting personal data before selling your vehicle. Yet this and inferred privacy policies were not easily found. In contrast, Tesla's online provisions were extremely clear and organised to minimise information fatigue.

Table 2. Comparison of the chosen vehicle's characteristics.

Make	Model	Date	Class	Power type	Market Capitalisation Rank [34]	Innovation Rank [33]
Audi	A6	2021	Executive	Conventional or Plug-in Hybrid	3rd	1st
BMW	i3 Electric	2015	Small Family	Electric	8th	4th
Ford	Focus	2021	Small Family	Mild Hybrid	15th	8th
Tesla	Model 3	2021	Large Family	Electric	1st	3rd
Toyota	Corolla	2020	Small Family	Conventional or Hybrid	2nd	13th
Volvo	XC40	2021	Small Off-road	Mild Hybrid or Electric	14th	9th

4   Assessing Consumer Awareness

This section describes the assessment process examined through a survey and focus group. The qualitive results were coded and analysed by a single researcher using Braun and Clarke's [35] six 'Phases of Thematic Analysis' to structure the process with minimal risk of bias. A primarily inductive analysis method was used to allow for data-driven results without a pre-existing coding framework, although aspects of deductive analysis were required to ensure the themes' relevance [36]. By combining both latent and semantic approaches to identifying meanings in data, explicit and underlying assumptions held by respondents can be equally recognised and merited, allowing wider contextual influences to give rich insight into the quantitative survey results [35]. The approach chosen reveals how consumers understand privacy in the context of their vehicles and if current provisions are effective or influential.

Manual coding was initially used to determine the broad ideas generated by the survey. The most frequent key words and phrases were collated and ordered by theme and frequency before being latently analysed for underlying themes, informing the questions asked in the focus group. An example of this is the high frequency of the keyword 'what', which was found 24 times in the initial manual coding, revealing uncertainties surrounding vehicular data collection. To understand this further, the focus group were asked to reflect on what influenced their ideas about the types of data collected. This exposed assumptions about the functions of modern vehicles and the ubiquitous use of sensors, which the participants did not expect vehicles to be capable of or that manufacturers were legally allowed to collect.

The manual coding method was replaced by NVivo 12 Pro software as the themes became more numerous and difficult to track. The software enabled a better adhesion to the six 'Phases of Thematic Analysis' and flexible, detailed thematic hierarchical organisation [35]. It allowed cross-examination between the survey and focus group coding, enabling a greater understanding of the cross-prevalence of themes and an insight into the influences that informed the quantitative survey results. Hierarchical organisation allowed broader, overarching themes to be established without losing the distinctions within each sub-theme, enabling multiple layers of specificity and coding [37]. This method preserved divergent responses which is imperative to creating a comprehensive benchmark that accurately reflects the market CAVs are entering.

4.1 Consumer Survey

An online consumer survey, titled 'Surveying Vehicular Data Privacy and the Consumer', was designed to liaise with the public as stakeholders and consisted of seven sections: the participant information sheet, demographic details, the respondent's primary vehicle, privacy in relation to the primary vehicle, general privacy questions, improving current privacy provisions, and contact information for joining the virtual focus group. Each section was designed to evaluate the consumer's awareness of CAV features in their own vehicles, their recognition of vehicular data collection, their experience of current privacy provisions and materials from manufacturers, and what is important to improving the consumer's engagement with their data privacy.

Survey Thematic Structure. Demographic information, including age, gender, and country of residence, was collected to understand the reach, possible overrepresentation bias, and generational impact that might be present in the responses, particularly with varying access to CAV technologies. Question branching was used to ensure the survey was asking suitable questions (e.g. not asking about experiences of manufacturer's privacy policies if they had answered 'No' or 'I am unsure of what that is' to the question 'Are you aware of what a privacy policy is?'). This filtering was also used to check if respondents were legally able to drive, currently drive, were resident in a country where GDPR is applicable, or knew what a privacy policy is, so that only suitable questions were asked. If they currently drive then generic information about the respondents' primary vehicle was collected, including the manufacturer, approximate vehicle age, fuel type, and transmission. Vehicle age indicated if the respondents might soon be replacing their vehicle for one with CAV features or already had them fitted. Respondents who drive were asked if they had changed their in-vehicle privacy settings to determine privacy uncertainty or engagement. They were similarly asked what level they had read their vehicle handbook to establish if it was used as a source of information and about the features their vehicle included to determine if CAV features are present in the respondents' primary vehicles, and how certain respondents were about the features their vehicles contain. Similarly, all respondents were asked which data types they believed were collected by manufacturers from modern vehicles. All the features listed in both questions were reported by manufacturers as used for data collection in their provided materials. The focus group then interrogated the presumptions that may have informed these answers.

Following the lack of clarity found in Table 1 surrounding how to remove personal data and who is responsible for vehicular updates, respondents were asked if they knew, as well as what they considered most important regarding manufacturers using their data, if manufacturer's current privacy provisions were sufficient, and how privacy information should be communicated. These questions revealed if the current provisions are effective, engaging, or are provided in the most appropriate places.

The primary question type used was multiple choice with option shuffling to minimise bias. In the full survey there also featured three dropdown, two matrix, and two open-ended questions, as well as options for the entry of an 'Other' option where appropriate. Open-ended and matrix questions were minimised to reduce fatigue and drop-out, ensuring the survey was not excessively long or complex to complete, but that it enabled the broadest spectrum of views to be expressed. Respondents were given an optional opportunity at the end of the survey to leave additional comments.

Survey Recruitment. The survey received ethics approval from the University of Nottingham before initiating. Participation was voluntary and relied on the respondent providing data. All responses were anonymous, and no personal data was collected. Respondents were recruited from social media (WhatsApp, Instagram, and Facebook), where the survey link was advertised from the researcher's account. Convenience sampling was primarily used to find respondents alongside snowballing sampling as respondents forwarded on the survey to friends and family. The survey was created using Microsoft Forms from the researcher's account to hold the results securely with the University of Nottingham's Office365 OneDrive. The survey was made available for desktop and mobile devices. A participant information sheet was provided at the beginning of the survey requiring the respondent's consent before continuing. No financial reward was given on completion, but respondents were invited to contact the researcher via email to join the focus group.

Pilot Survey. Before conducting the primary survey, a pilot was used to evaluate the clarity, effectiveness, and time taken to complete the survey. Consisting of 27 questions, the pilot was completed from 2nd August 2021 to 3rd August 2021 by 7 respondents from 9 asked and took an average of 16 min and 21 s to complete. Respondent feedback resulted in an extension of the estimated survey completion time from 10 min to 10–15 min and included multiple revisions such as altering the wording of the open-ended question 'What would help you take control of your data?' to 'What would help you feel in control of your data?' to remove the implication that the data collected is out of the consumer's control. The pilot also revealed a need to prepare for the unexpected after an unintended situation occurred after one respondent spent an hour on the survey whilst they read their owner's handbook to respond to a question about their vehicle's features.

Primary Survey. The primary consumer survey of 28 questions was conducted from 5th August 2021 to 19th August 2021, receiving 168 responses with an average completion time of 18 min 12 s. Respondents were from 14 countries, with the majority (130 respondents) from the United Kingdom due to this being the country in which the study originated and where the majority of the researcher's contacts resided. Significant over-representation of the age category '21–40 years old' occurred, with 131 respondents selecting this age. These disproportionate representations may result in bias that must be acknowledged. 61% of respondents identified as female, 38% as male, and 1% as non-binary. As there were only three responses to a follow-up question for those who had read their privacy policy about their experience of it, its results were omitted due to insufficient data.

Survey Limitations. The survey did not gather enough data from countries other than the United Kingdom to fully examine cross-cultural differences that may influence the results. The personality traits and demographic details of respondents across multiple countries has already been studied by Kyriakidis, Happee, and de Winter [38], determining differences between public opinion about autonomous vehicles, including privacy concerns although in less depth than in this paper. The survey does not consider manufacturer's mobile apps, data stored on such apps, or the collection of financial/ID details for financing or internet connectivity services, as these were considered to exceed the scope of the paper. A consideration of respondent bias as a result of limited exposure to CAVs, as identified by Liu, Nikitas, and Parkison [9], must be acknowledged as this may manifest in forms such as optimism bias and lack of awareness bias that may influence responses to the survey. This survey did not collect data regarding the respondents' previous experience of CAVs.

4.2 Focus Group

To complement the survey findings, a small focus group was used to expand upon and investigate further the identified themes, generating a more detailed insight into consumer knowledge, differing from the interviews of CAV experts conducted by Liu et al. [9]. The content of the focus group was semi-structured around key questions, developed from the data of the initial survey results, and a supporting presentation. The focus group began with open questions and gradually increased in structure whilst allowing for spontaneous pursual of any points raised. The primary limitation of the focus group was that only one was run and therefore the number of views gathered may be representative of only a snapshot of consumer understanding. However, the themes arising from the focus group, in combination with the survey findings are together substantial and significant, complimenting the breadth of the survey with the detail and depth of the shared consumer experiences in the focus group.

Focus Group Structure. Participants were shown a screenshot of the question and options for the survey question 'Which of the following do you believe are collected by manufacturers from modern vehicles?' and were told the three options least chosen from the survey results. They were asked what had influenced their decision about which data types would or would not be collected by manufacturers. This question was designed to unpick the assumptions and beliefs held by consumers about the vehicles they currently drive and to understand how they define a vehicle's functionality. In response to the group's discussion, an additional question was asked about how the participants felt about driving a car that collected all the data listed. Participants were also asked for practical solutions on how consumers could be better engaged with their privacy in ways that they themselves would use given that the survey revealed that only 5% of drivers who knew what a privacy policy was had read their vehicle manufacturer's privacy policy. Following the suggestions of in-vehicle solutions, the group was asked if in-vehicle privacy settings or notifications could be better used to convey privacy information to users. After a discussion revealing the high likelihood that such notifications would be ignored if they were in-vehicle and a further unpicking of what the participants understood a vehicle to be, the use of a manufacturer's app as a way of engaging consumers with privacy was suggested. The final question of the focus group was scenario based, comparing a non-CAV vehicle and a vehicle with CAV features. Participants were asked which of the vehicles they would drive depending on three different features and risks: Connectivity, Data access, and Connected Safety features. With each of these factors participants were challenged to discuss why they had chosen a specific vehicle and what would change their mind. This exercise was used to determine if consumers value their privacy when offered new features by vehicle manufacturers in exchange for their consumer data.

Focus Group Recruitment. The focus group received ethics approval from the University of Nottingham before initiating and was hosted online due to the Coronavirus pandemic. Participants were recruited from the survey, researcher's social media account using convenience sampling, and using snowballing sampling as participants passed the focus group details to friends and family. Seven interested participants were sent an information sheet and consent form, with six responding with completed paperwork. Participation was voluntary with no financial reward and the meeting's video, audio, and transcript were recorded and anonymised. The focus group was conducted over Microsoft Teams via the researcher's account to securely store the recorded meeting and transcript on the University of Nottingham's OneDrive.

Participant Characteristics. The focus group was conducted on 21st August 2021 with 6 participants and lasted 1 h 15 min. Written and verbal consent was given by all participants. Contrasting the over-representation of female identifying survey respondents, most of the focus group participants identified as male, with only one participant identifying as female. All were from different backgrounds and professions, including business, environmental science, the vehicle manufacturing industry, two students from sciences, and one of humanities. None of the participants were experts in CAVs.

Analysis Method. Following Braun & Clarke's [35]'15-Point Checklist of Criteria for Good Thematic Analysis', the transcription automatically generated by Microsoft Teams was first checked against the original video recording of the meeting for correctness and 'accuracy' as described by 'Process 1'. The transcript was anonymised of all identifying data so that the participants could not be recognized from the text. Areas where multiple participants spoke simultaneously were marked and the dialogue pieced together where this had occurred. Nvivo 12 Pro was then used to organise the focus group transcript using nodes for each question and each question's responses were coded. Resulting themes identified in the responses were created as child nodes of these questions. Any responses that contrasted or departed from the group consensus were not discarded, ensuring that the full spectrum of views was gathered as described in process 2 and 3 [35]. Themes present in multiple questions were merged as part of the refinement process. Word frequency queries were used to visualise the coded questions, revealing phrases and words that signposted to themes mentioned most often. This tool was used to check overall coherence of the identified themes and to ensure no encoding had been missed. Once the primary coding stage was completed and the themes were checked against the original uncoded transcript, examples were chosen to best illustrate each of the identified themes. These examples were then combined into the detailed analysis following processes 4 through to 10, whilst maintaining an active approach to analysis and coding as emphasised by process 15 [35].

5   Results

This section details and discusses the thematically analysed results of the consumer survey and focus group, which incorporate quantitative survey results to support the primary qualitive thematic analysis. It is organised into themes or by question.

5.1   Consumer Survey

Of the 168 respondents of the survey 69% drive a vehicle. Despite only 8% of drivers reporting that current privacy provisions are sufficient, only 5% of respondents who say they drive a vehicle with privacy settings have changed their in-vehicle settings, whilst the remaining 95% of respondents report never having changed or looked at such settings. 29% of respondents did not know if their vehicle had this optionality. As only 14% of drivers had read and 52% partially read their vehicle handbook, many may be unaware that such privacy controls exist. Groups with particularly low engagement with their vehicle handbook included drivers who neither own nor lease the primary vehicle they drive and those who drive monthly or less frequently than monthly. These two groups consisted of over 95% of respondents aged younger than 40 years who drove a high proportion of primary vehicles aged between 6 and 10 years old. Despite the lack of engagement with the owner's manual, it was the second most popular place (33%) respondents aware of what a privacy policy is said they would look for privacy information. Those who owned their primary vehicle and those who drive weekly were more likely to read a vehicle handbook.

Drivers who lease their primary vehicle or drivers who have over 20 years of driving experience had the highest respective proportions of vehicles aged less than 3 years old, and therefore are the most likely to be exposed to CAV features. Both respondents who drive monthly or less frequently than monthly and those who own the primary vehicle that they drive had the highest proportion of respondents who felt that the current privacy provisions were insufficient or were unsure. In contrast, the three respondents who had read their vehicle manufacturer's privacy policy were drivers who drive daily and owned their primary vehicle. Whilst daily drivers, when comparing driving frequency, were the most likely to be aware of what a privacy policy is they were also the most likely to never look at or change their in-vehicle settings.

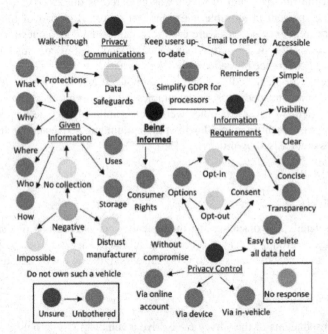

Fig. 1. Thematic map of responses to 'What would help you feel in control of your data?' [1].

'WHat Would Help You Feel in Control of Your Data?'. The primary overarching theme of the open-ended question 'What would help you feel in control of your data?', was that respondents needed to be 'Informed'. Two respondents gave no response, with one noting that they were "not overly bothered about what vehicle data is recorded by the manufacturer". There were 9 negative responses, ranging from it is impossible to feel in control of your data to the only solution is not to own a CAV as "I drive a car to go from A to B, not to supply data to others". 13 respondents expressed uncertainty about being able to be in control, one noting "I'm not sure it's possible to feel in control of data collected". The remaining 85% of responses relate to the themes of 'Given Information',

'Information Requirements', 'Privacy Communications', and 'Privacy Control', which are summarised in Fig. 1 and discussed below in more detail.

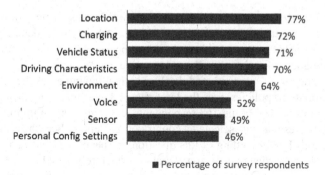

Location 77%
Charging 72%
Vehicle Status 71%
Driving Characteristics 70%
Environment 64%
Voice 52%
Sensor 49%
Personal Config Settings 46%

■ Percentage of survey respondents

Fig. 2. Data that respondents believe is collected by manufacturers from modern vehicles [1].

Given Information. 55% of responses to the question 'What would help you feel in control of your data?' were concerned with the given privacy information and how this impacted their ability to feel in control. 35% of all respondents wanted the information provided to specifically address how their data is being used, where it is stored, who has access to it, and why and what is being collected. When asked which data types are collected (Fig. 2), the most chosen type was location data (77%). When similarly asked about the features present in their primary vehicle, the 'built-in SIM' feature had the highest level of uncertainty (43% responded with "I don't know"), with an average of 17% of respondents being unsure about any of the listed features. 19% of drivers reported their vehicle had none of the listed features, although 95% of these drivers had a primary vehicle aged 6 years old or older and therefore their vehicle may reasonably not have such features. Drivers with a vehicle aged 5 years old or newer had a particularly high rate of uncertainty about the data collecting features of their vehicle, answering with "I don't know" to 23% of the listed features. When comparing driving frequency, those who drive monthly or less frequently answered "I don't know" to 27% of the listed features. Respondents with over 20 years of driving experience were the most certain about their vehicle's features, answering "I don't know" to 9% of the features. No respondents reported having a primary vehicle with all listed features. This uncertainty correlates with 20% of respondents who wanted to know what data was being collected.

10% of respondents, the second largest group of participants who were concerned about the specific information provided, wanted to be given detailed information about how the collected data is used. This included the safeguards in place to protect all data transmitted or stored to increase confidence in the manufacturer. One participant suggested that manufacturers should provide "greater assurance that legislation is followed" to combat this mistrust in vehicle manufacturers. Whilst 82% of respondents who are resident in the UK have heard of the term 'GDPR' (General Data Protection Regulation), another participant suggested that "Few data processors understand the requirements under GDPR" and "Perhaps a simplification of the legislation" would be required "so that data processors understand what their obligations are" and this can then provide greater clarity in the given privacy information for consumers. This survey did not measure the data processor's understanding of GDPR and so this response could not be followed up with more information.

Information Requirements. 39% of respondents noted the specific requirements that manufacturers must meet for consumers to feel in control of their data. Privacy information must be visible and accessible to the consumer from the manufacturer's website, written clearly and concisely in "layman's terms" using "simple language and expression" without the use of "jargon", and disclosed when buying a vehicle. Despite these responses, 'Brevity of policies' was the least chosen factor regarding data use by manufacturers with only 20% of the 168 respondents regarding it as an important factor to them. As 90% of respondents selected a country of residence where the official national language is English, the wording of this question has been ruled out as a cause of this factor's low selection. Respondents noted that manufacturers must be "more open when selling you the car to what your car is collecting from you" and that consumers should be "given a document detailing it all on purchase of the vehicle", including information about consumer rights in relation to data collection and privacy. Transparency was prioritised by 77% of respondents and specified by 12% as crucial for them to take control of their data.

Privacy Communications. 10% of responses placed emphasis on keeping consumers up-to-date and informed about data privacy to help them feel more in control of their data. This includes notifying consumers through reminders and "in car prompts" to check their privacy settings or explain changes in the vehicle manufacturer's data privacy provisions. One respondent suggested the benefits of having "An email to refer back to". Respondents proposed a privacy information walk-through and stressed the importance of "Being able to discuss policies with someone" with "Clear step-by-step breakdowns" of the information. When consulted about how privacy information should be communicated to the consumer, the most preferred method was via email (74%). Whilst 43% preferred the information via in-vehicle updates, only 8% of the drivers who knew what a privacy policy is said they would look for it in-vehicle via the infotainment system. 35% noted that they would check the website instead. Two respondents suggested receiving this information via a mobile phone app (1%), which was the preferred method of the focus group participants who expanded further on the benefits and disadvantages of using these different methods of communication (see Sect. 5.2). Despite websites being the preferred communication method of a third of the respondents, only 3 respondents checked it.

Privacy Control. 48% of respondents needed control over what data is gathered to feel in control, including the "ability to completely opt out of data collection without loss of function" or "reduced user experience". Such privacy controls may include an "Easy option to clear all held data (e.g. single button press)". Respondents expressed the need for multiple places they can control their privacy from, such as in the vehicle, from a mobile device, and/or from an online account, so that they can give "informed and specific consent" including the "right automatically not to share your data". 26% of respondents specifically noted the need for opt-in or opt-out options, which corresponds with 70% of respondents prioritising 'Clear opt-out information' as the second most important factor of their data use by vehicle manufacturers.

'Do you have any further comments?'. The final survey question, an optional open-ended response question, received 27 responses representing 16% of all respondents. These further comments generally reflect the survey's results, noting the underestimation consumers have about the data collection and privacy control functionalities of the vehicles they drive. Whilst 28% of the primary vehicles were 11 years old or older and may currently only include few of the listed features, the average age of a vehicle at scrappage is only 13.9 years and therefore these drivers may soon be replacing their vehicle with one that may have such features [29]. Respondents who noted that their vehicle is too old for privacy concerns to be applicable to them, for example if they have a vehicle that "does not have the technology for me to enter personal data", may need extra support in transferring to the highly technical nature of new vehicles, as well as understanding the features and privacy controls that they may be unaware of existing. Respondents expressed how they had not thought of privacy and data collection in relation to their vehicles before, as vehicles previously did not have such inherent capabilities which computers and mobile phones may be thought of as synonymous with. Such respondents commented that "The survey clearly illustrates how little I know about my car" and that "These very questions raise my awareness level and concern regarding personal data collected by my car!" suggesting that the survey may have been the first point some respondents had been informed that modern vehicles collect data. This concerning pattern is further explored by the focus group (see Sect. 5.2). One respondent went as far as describing how "Whilst I have provided data on my more recent vehicle - it is to no small extent why I choose to maintain vehicles with NO data collection provision at all. Even to the extent of vehicles without electronics" due to the "implications of data theft and misuse" as well as the "not insignificant risk of unsolicited access (hacking)" if "remote access/update" is not "controlled – and IMO prohibited".

5.2 Focus Group

The four key themes, summarised in Fig. 3, were identified from the focus group as: 'Disinterest', 'Distrust', 'Impact', and 'Vehicle Perception'.

Disinterest. Participants express that disinterest forms from two distinct branches. The first is that consumers are uninterested in their data privacy due to the technical wording and length of the current policies. This correlates with the survey results, where only 57% of respondents who drive know what a privacy policy is, and of those only 3 participants had read their vehicle's. Of the 116 respondents who drive, only 2 had changed their in-vehicle privacy settings. One participant noted how they were surprised of other's deep consideration about their privacy, as they had "never thought people really cared about their data protection as much". Two participants admitted to not reading privacy policies for these reasons. One participant suggested "a summary sheet sort of thing, because obviously policies are usually a fair few pages long" that gives "a general overview of things" similar to "when you're at uni you've always got an abstract at the start". This, in conjunction with better navigation through the policy, was proposed as a method that would encourage them to read the privacy policy where they had not previously. One participant expanded on this, suggesting that "other methods such as audio or video within the vehicles, panels or consoles could be used to essentially make the new owners of the vehicles more interested into this information", for example when getting "into the vehicle for the first time" as part of "a vehicle setup". This could be specifically targeted towards new CAV drivers, including the "the possible consequences of logging that information".

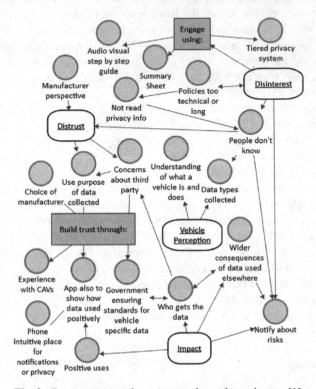

Fig. 3. Focus group results represented as a thematic map [1].

Whilst these approaches addressed new vehicle ownership, further suggestions considered how to actively engage consumers in the long term rather than passively through a one-time setting selection. One participant suggested a form of "tiered system" for privacy settings, similar to that used for cookies on websites, where each tier relates according to personal attitudes towards risk. Each tier gives examples of what is transmitted at each level, so that each consumer can choose the "level of data collection are you comfortable with". The use of vehicle manufacturers' apps as a platform was suggested as "people usually tend to check their phones quite frequently" as it is perceived as a more native environment for notifications and data privacy, whereas a vehicle has not been the traditional place to expect data privacy to be a concern. One participant further explained this as "people will, you know, sit and access their phone from anywhere, whereas you're not always necessarily going to sit in your car like you're going into your car you're going somewhere". This disengagement and disinterest with privacy because of the traditional definition of a vehicle was also described by another participant: "I think they're going to be more likely to check what that notification is about, rather than you know, seeing a notification on the cars dashboard and thinking like, oh, there's something wrong with my vehicle". This raised discussion about "you see all sorts of jokes about how difficult it is just to change the clock in your car, let alone you know, go through and find the privacy settings". Participants also shared their personal experiences of drivers ignoring the warning lights currently used in vehicles to communicate faults or issues requiring maintenance. Therefore, despite 43% of the survey participants choosing in-vehicle updates as the preferred method of communicating privacy information to the consumer, this method may in practice fail to engage consumers in the long term.

The second form of disinterest in data privacy expressed by participants is caused if a consumer has not been touched by the effects of their data being misused. If the consumer is not a person at risk of harm if their data was to be leaked or taken advantage of, then they may not take the need for privacy provisions seriously. One participant described how their reluctance towards CAVs partially stems from having "grown up knowing what the risks are with cyber". This background informed their decision to choose a non-CAV vehicle in the vehicle comparison scenario, even with the additional features CAVs may provide. Participants of the focus group discussed the need for transparency, honesty, and frankness about the potential risks involved as a way of motivating consumers, as well as requiring the vehicle manufacturers to show what is being done to protect consumers' data. One participant described how "when I usually get into a car, I don't think you know that somebody could, I don't know, use the GPS system of my car to track where I am and then stalk me afterwards. You know, like people just think, oh, you know there's a car I can drive from point A to point B. They don't even think that you know a car could be having any like computers inside of it". The disjointed relationship between the modern, connected vehicle and the self-contained, unconnected vehicle the participants have grown up with contributes to the belief that privacy concerns are not relevant for end-users. The potential risks of CAVs discussed here intersect with the theme 'Impact'.

Distrust. Participants identified a significant source of distrust in manufacturers and third parties as a major influence on consumer privacy engagement. The survey found that only 5% of respondents felt that the current privacy provisions from vehicle manufacturers were sufficient and 78% were unsure if these sufficient. Of the 8 respondents representing the 5%, 4 had not read their primary vehicle manufacturer's privacy policy and 3 did not know what one was. These statistics reveal a significant and inhibiting lack of consumer awareness and education. The focus group participants were concerned about the extent of data gathered from consumers and their vehicles: "I'm not sure how pleased I'd be about a private, you know, a private entity like a company collecting all that level of data 'cause it's just a little bit [...] invasive in a way, and it sort of does beg the question, where would they then stop? If you don't, I mean in terms of how much they want to be involved in our lives."

Participants discussed the implications of companies knowing about a consumer's interests, journeys, and routines for the purposes of personalised marketing. Two participants expressed that "as long as the manufacturer is ensuring that the data is safe" they were unconcerned about the manufacturer's access to their data. Another participant was more concerned about other entities obtaining their data but resolved that "you can also choose your manufacturer so there is a little bit of choice there about which company you go to". This implies that certain manufacturers may be considered more trustworthy over another, and that a manufacturer's record may play a larger role in CAV purchasing decisions. One participant, who works for a vehicle manufacturer, expressed how manufacturers "are incredibly paranoid about any data leaking out because it would be obviously massive reputational damage if it happened". Another participant felt that their attitude towards data sharing "would depend on who's using it in a strange way [...] who they decide to pass it onto".

To combat this distrust, one participant wanted to see the government step in with vehicular data specific regulations and guidance beyond GDPR to give the public confidence that manufacturers are protecting consumer data, especially when giving third parties data access. This government assurance would increase public trust, adding a further layer of protection, creating a "two step policy rather than one step policy". By "notifying participants and directly displaying to them how their data is used" through "early intervention" and not just as "a response to the problems", the participant's distrust may be reduced. Two participants agreed that using the manufacturer's app in this way would be helpful. By encouraging data usage transparency and allowing the consumer access to the data collected about them, the consumer can see that the data shared directly improves their consumer experience.

Impact. When discussing the negative and positive realities of sharing vehicular data, one participant expressed concern about the interdependence of systems on data shared by vehicles, such as voice data. If "people could essentially get the audio signatures of the voice commands collected [then it] could be used maliciously to access other data which is hidden behind voice commands" such as the use of voice ID as an authentication method to access banking over-the-phone or online. Another concern raised by this participant was that they would be "more worried, let's say if a specific company was working with a specific government". Another participant was concerned that vehicular data may be used to track individuals seen by the state as a threat. When choosing a vehicle manufacturer based on their reputation, "you think the company is trustworthy, but in other countries the company could be very corrupt, and they could be well working with the government to give away your data to them". Another participant reflected on this attitude "that the government is like we're just going to assume that you've done something wrong, even if you know you're perfectly trustworthy individual that's broken the law in your life." They explained that this doesn't "leave the best impression on your sort of populist does it [...] going well I'm going to track you anyway". Another participant added that the lives of those under witness protection or being stalked may be at risk should their vehicular data be intercepted. In this scenario protections must be in place for vulnerable CAV users.

The positive impact of sharing vehicular data with manufacturers was also discussed. One participant gave the example of the eCall system, which has "saved lives already", where vehicle sensor data is used "to detect if the vehicle's been in an accident" and "alert emergency authorities". Another participant felt that the benefits of CAVs and sharing vehicular data could only be gained "if all of the cars are on the same system" but was prepared to relinquish their privacy "once I was confident that it would be better for everyone's safety". One participant spoke of the positive impact of lower maintenance costs and the ease of handsfree communication integration. Two participants expressed that as they had grown up with their parents driving non-CAVs they felt more hesitant about CAVs. Both participants strongly chose a CAV over a non-CAV when given the option. Conversely, a different participant said they felt more comfortable with CAVs because they had grown up with one in the family.

Vehicle Perception. The uncertainty about vehicular data collection originates in vehicles only recently becoming connected and transmitting the data they collect rather than purely using it for the operation of in-vehicle systems. What was an isolated system is now part of a pervasive range of integrated data collection technologies able to connect with other vehicles, infrastructure, and/or manufacturers. The consumer's understanding of this has not caught up with the fast pace of vehicle development, with associations of CAVs being limited to futuristic, expensive, or "flashy" vehicles. One participant noted that the "ordinary consumer" may decide that "if I see that [a] vehicle seems nicer to me, then perhaps the privacy and all the data and stuff is not that much of an important factor anymore if I don't know much about it." Another participant expressed that when completing the survey, they thought ""I don't think they could collect that" then moved on, possibly a little naively". One participant considered that the data types listed legally may or "may not be allowed to be collected". Other participants expressed uncertainty at first, but then considered what data would be useful if collected from the manufacturer's perspective and on reflection discussed what influenced their underestimation. One participant felt that when completing the survey "I wasn't sure how they would get that data. And having looked at the list again, I think I've now worked out how each one would be collected".

6   Conclusions and Recommendations

CAVs encompass more than a clearly defined product. They are representative of a scale of disruptive, pervasive, and integrated technologies that are present in vehicles both on the market and on the road, as well as those in concept. It is critical that the consumer's perception and understanding of what a vehicle is and does is addressed by the industry. There is a disjointed relationship between the self-contained and unconnected vehicle that the respondents have experienced and the increasing connectivity of vehicles on the market. As evidenced by the results of this paper, consumers understand CAVs to be futuristic or expensive vehicles that are not currently on the road. This mythology surrounding CAVs and their features only fuels the belief that vehicular privacy is not a consideration required of a vehicle, as it has not been previously. Survey respondents demonstrated that they struggle to identify the technologies that collect data in their primary vehicles and underestimate the categories of data that vehicle manufacturers may collect. This uncertainty is also found concerning what data is and is not legally allowed to be collected by manufacturers. When purchasing a vehicle information about its data collection activities and privacy controls must be available. The manufacturer must make the consumer aware of how to remove personal data, change privacy settings, find privacy information, and told who to contact regarding privacy questions or concerns. An in-vehicle and/or in-app walkthrough of the data transmitting features and privacy settings is recommended for all consumers purchasing a vehicle with CAV features, particularly given the low engagement with current provisions revealed in this paper. Manufacturers must demonstrate protections are in place for end-users at high risk if their identity or location can be obtained.

A joint industry and government education campaign, which includes CAV experience for the public, is recommended to aid the adoption of and trust in CAVs. This is particularly important for those with no experience of such vehicles and their functionality, as this paper evidences that they are the most cautious group of consumers towards CAVs. These users will need extra support in adapting to the highly technical nature of CAVs, as well as understanding the features and privacy controls that they may be unaware of and will benefit best from a walkthrough of the vehicle's features.

The government could usefully provide vehicular data specific regulations and guidance, including frameworks beyond the current GDPR provisions. This must address how consumers' data is being used, where it is stored, who has access to it, why their data is being collected, and what data is being collected from their vehicle. This information must be clearly visible and accessible from the manufacturer's website, written in simple language and expression with clear explanations, examples, and summaries of their policies towards data privacy. Transparency must be at the core of the information provided and written with the consumer as the target audience. The information supplied should be easily navigated through to prevent information fatigue. Vehicle manufacturers must assure consumers that they follow the legislation, as their cyber security and data privacy record will, as evidenced by this paper's results, play a large role in the consumer's consideration of which CAV to purchase.

Consumers must be able to make informed choices about their data privacy through upfront honest and transparent communications with manufacturers about the benefits and risks of sharing their data. By allowing the consumer access to the data collected about them, the consumer can see that sharing their data directly improves their consumer experience. They must be kept up-to-date and informed by, for example, being allowed access to vehicular software update notes. Despite 58% of drivers who are aware of what a privacy policy is said they would look for privacy information on their vehicle manufacturer's website and 33% would look in the vehicle handbook, this paper finds that these sources of information are insufficient at engaging and educating the consumer. The use of in-vehicle solutions also failed to engage consumers with their privacy in the long term as focus group participants expressed that this was because a vehicle is associated with going somewhere and that the currently used warning light system often goes ignored. The manufacturer's mobile application was identified by the focus group participants as the most native environment for notifications about data privacy. This paper recommends that the app should be used to engage consumers actively, not passively, with their data privacy by allowing the consumer to see exactly how their data is being used. To maximise flexibility and accessibility, privacy controls should still be available in multiple places, such as in-vehicle or via an online account. An opt-in, tiered system of privacy controls based on risk levels is recommended. There must be no penalty for reduced data collection, either as a reduced user experience or substantial loss of vehicle functionality.

6.1 Limitations and Future Work

The survey conducted only considered data being collected (including remotely) and used by the vehicle manufacturer and third parties. Future work may consider the data stored in-vehicle, on the manufacturer's mobile app, and on associated apps used in the infotainment system. Also, this survey does not examine the impact of mobile apps as a way of accessing privacy information, although this was discussed by the focus group as a potential solution to improving access and engagement with current privacy provisions. When reflecting on other solutions to engage consumers with their vehicular data privacy, future work may consider examining how other fields are attempting to engage the public with their cyber security and study if any such approaches may address the barriers respondents raised in this paper. Future research may also be conducted into mapping the changing data and privacy knowledge of consumers through repeating the survey and focus group at periodic intervals in the future, especially as CAVs become more commonplace on the road.

References

1. Barber, F., Furnell, S.: Benchmarking consumer data and privacy knowledge in connected and autonomous vehicles. In: 8th International Conference on Information Systems Security and Privacy - ICISSP, pp. 426–434. SciTePress (2022). https://doi.org/10.5220/001086200 0003120
2. Boom, F.: If Autonomous cars could talk! 135 Privacy Laws Bus. Int. **17**, 17 (2015)
3. Bertoncello, M., et al.: Monetizing Car Data. McKinsey & Company (2016). https://www.mckinsey.com/industries/automotiveand-assembly/our-insights/monetizing-car-data. Accessed 09 June 2021
4. Karnouskos, S., Kerschbaum, F.: Privacy and integrity considerations in hyperconnected autonomous vehicles. Proc. IEEE **106**(1), 160–170 (2018). https://doi.org/10.1109/JPROC.2017.2725339
5. Strandberg, K., Olovsson, T., Jonsson, E.: Securing the connected car. IEEE Veh. Technol. Mag. **13**(1), 56–65 (2018). https://doi.org/10.1109/MVT.2017.2758179
6. Bradbury, M., Taylor, P., Atmaca, U.I., Maple, C., Griffiths, N.: Privacy challenges with protecting live vehicular location context. IEEE Access **8**, 207465–207484 (2020). https://doi.org/10.1109/ACCESS.2020.3038533
7. Dean, B.C.: Three Core Security & Privacy Issues of Connected Vehicles. Center for Democracy & Technology (2017).https://cdt.org/insights/three-coresecurity-privacy-issues-of-connected-vehicles/. Accessed 09 June 2021
8. Nikitas, A., Michalakopoulou, K., Njoya, E.T., Karampatzakis, D.: Artificial intelligence, transport and the smart city: definitions and dimensions of a new mobility era. Sustainability **12**(7), 2789. MDPI AG (2020). https://doi.org/10.3390/su12072789
9. Liu, N., Nikitas, A., Parkinson, S.: Exploring expert perceptions about the cyber security and privacy of connected and autonomous vehicles: a thematic analysis approach. Transp. Res. Part F: Traff. Psychol. Behav. **75**, 66–86 (2020). https://doi.org/10.1016/j.trf.2020.09.019

10. Maeng, K., Kim, W., Cho, Y.: Consumers' attitudes toward information security threats against connected and autonomous vehicles. Telematics Inform. **63** (2021). https://doi.org/10.1016/j.tele.2021.101646

11. Enev, M., Takakuwa, A., Koscher, K., Kohno, T.: Automobile driver fingerprinting. Proc. Privacy Enhanc. Technol. **2016**(1), 34–51 (2015). https://doi.org/10.1515/popets-2015-0029

12. Virojboonkiate, N., Vateekul, P., Rojviboonchai, K.: Driver identification using histogram and neural network from acceleration data. In: 17th IEEE International Conference on Communication Technology, pp. 1560–1564 (2017). https://doi.org/10.1109/ICCT.2017.8359893

13. Pesé, M.D., Shin, K.G.: Survey of automotive privacy regulations and privacy-related attacks. In: SAE Technical Paper Series (2019). https://doi.org/10.4271/2019-01-0479

14. Butt, T.A., Iqbal, R., Salah, K., Aloqaily, M., Jararweh, Y.: Privacy management in social internet of vehicles: review, challenges and blockchain based solutions. IEEE Access **7**, 79694–79713 (2019). https://doi.org/10.1109/ACCESS.2019.2922236

15. Bellatti, J., et al.: Driving habits data: location privacy implications and solutions. IEEE Secur. Privacy **15**(1), 12–20 (2017). https://doi.org/10.1109/MSP.2017.6

16. Beato, G.: Google's driverless future: will self-piloting vehicles rob us of the last of our privacy and autonomy? Reason (2013). https://reason.com/2013/05/10/googles-driverless-future/. Accessed 09 June 2021

17. Collingwood, L.: Privacy implications and liability issues of autonomous vehicles. In: Inf. Commun. Technol. Law **26**(1), 32–45 (2017). https://doi.org/10.1080/13600834.2017.1269871

18. Glancy, D.J.: Privacy in autonomous vehicles. Santa Clara Law Rev. **52**(4), 1171–1239 (2012)

19. Cheah, M., Haynes, S., Wooderson, P.: Smart vehicles: the data privacy smog. In: IEEE SmartWorld, Ubiquitous Intelligence & Computing, Advanced & Trusted Computing, Scalable Computing & Communications, Cloud & Big Data Computing, Internet of People and Smart City Innovations, pp. 82–87 (2018). https://doi.org/10.1109/SmartWorld.2018.00049

20. Hamilton, B.A.: Driving away with your data: privacy and connected vehicles. In: United States Government Accountability Office: Report to the Subcommittee on Research and Technology, Committee on Science, Space, and Technology, House of Representatives, GAO-17-656 (2019). https://www.gao.gov/assets/gao-17-656.pdf. Accessed 09 June 2021

21. Prevost, S., Kettani, H.: On data privacy in modern personal vehicles. In: Proceedings of the 4th International Conference on Big Data and Internet of Things, pp. 1–4 (2019). https://doi.org/10.1145/3372938.3372940

22. Frassinelli, D., Park, S., Nürnberger, S.: I know where you parked last summer: automated reverse engineering and privacy analysis of modern cars. In: IEEE Symposium on Security and Privacy, pp. 1401–1415 (2020). https://doi.org/10.1109/SP40000.2020.00081

23. UNESC: Revised Framework document on automated/autonomous vehicles. In: World Forum for Harmonization of Vehicle Regulations, United Nations Economic and Social Council, 3 September 2019. https://unece.org/DAM/trans/doc/2019/wp29/ECE-TRANSWP29-2019-34-rev.1e.pdf. Accessed 25 May 2021

24. SMMT: Connected and Autonomous Vehicles: SMMT Position Paper. The Society of Motor Manufacturers and Traders Limited (2017). https://www.smmt.co.uk/wpcontent/uploads/sites/2/SMMT-CAV-position-paper-final.pdf. Accessed 21 May 2021

25. National Automobile Dealers Association and the Future of Privacy Forum: Personal Data In Your Car. https://fpf.org/wp-content/uploads/2017/01/consumerguide.pdf. Accessed 09 June 2021

26. Bryans, J.W.: The internet of automotive things: vulnerabilities, risks and policy implications. . Cyber Policy **2**(2), 185–194 (2017). https://doi.org/10.1080/23738871.2017.1360926

27. Kam, R.: Connected cars: security and privacy risks on wheels. IAPP. https://iapp.org/news/a/connected-cars-security-and-privacy-risks-on-wheels/. Accessed 09 June 2021

28. Joy, J., Gerla, M.: Internet of vehicles and autonomous connected car - privacy and security issues. UCLA (2017). https://escholarship.org/uc/item/7rp5604s. Accessed 09 June 2021

29. SMMT: 2021 Automotive Sustainability Report: Average Vehicle Age (2016). https://www. smmt.co.uk/industry-topics/sustainability/average-vehicle-age/. Accessed 09 June 2021

30. Ghane, S., Jolfaei, A., Kulik, L., Ramamohanarao, K., Puthal, D.: Preserving privacy in the internet of connected vehicles. IEEE Trans. Intell. Transp. Syst. 1–10 (2020). https://doi.org/10.1109/TITS.2020.2964410

31. Vitale, C.: The CARAMEL project: a secure architecture for connected and autonomous vehicles. In: 2020 European Conference on Networks and Communications (EuCNC), pp. 133–138 (2020). https://doi.org/10.1109/EuCNC48522.2020.9200945

32. 5StarS: A Roadmap to Resilience: How the Automotive Sector can build trust in Connected Vehicles. 5StarS White Paper (2019). https://5starsproject.com/wpcontent/uploads/2019/06/5StarS_WhitePaper_12_6_19.pdf. Accessed 09 June 2021

33. Centre of Automotive Management: AutomotiveINNOVATIONS: Ranking of the most innovative automotive OEMs and premium brands 2021. https://auto-institut.de/automotiveinnovations/automotiveinnovations-ranking-of-themost-innovative-automotive-oems-and-premium-brands-2021/. Accessed 09 June 2021

34. Ghosh, I.: The World's Top Car Manufacturers by Market Capitalization (2021). https://www.visualcapitalist.com/worlds-top-car-manufacturerby-market-cap/. Accessed 09 June 2021

35. Braun, V., Clarke, V.: Using thematic analysis in psychology. Qual. Res. Psychol. 3(2), 77–101 (2006). https://doi.org/10.1191/1478088706qp063oa

36. Byrne, D.: A worked example of Braun and Clarke's approach to reflexive thematic analysis. Qual. Quant. 56, 1–22 (2021). https://doi.org/10.1007/s11135-021-01182-y

37. Nowell, L., Norris, J., White, D., Moules, N.: Thematic analysis. Int. J. Qual. Methods 16(1), 1–13 (2017). https://doi.org/10.1177/1609406917733847

38. Kyriakidis, M., Happee, R., de Winter, J.: Public opinion on automated driving: results of an international questionnaire among 5000 respondents. Transp. Res. Part F Traff. Psychol. Behav. 32, 127–140 (2015). https://doi.org/10.1016/j.trf.2015.04.014

Improving Data Security and Privacy
for Ontology Based Data Access

Ozgu Can[✉][iD] and Murat Osman Unalir[iD]

Department of Computer Engineering, Ege University, 35100 Bornova-Izmir, Turkey
{ozgu.can,murat.osman.unalir}@ege.edu.tr

Abstract. Data integration is the process of combining data from multiple disparate source systems to provide users a unified view of data. Nevertheless, integrating and transforming data from various sources are significant challenges. Also, providing the semantics in data representation is an important issue to perform effective data analysis and visualization. In this context, ontology based approaches are used to provide an effective and flexible combination of data from multiple heterogeneous sources. Ontologies support more expressive representations and consistency for the data integration process. Ontology Based Data Access (OBDA) allows to map an ontology to a data source in order to query heterogeneous data more easier. Hence, data integration and data access are ensured with this mapping. As a result, large amounts of data can be stored more efficiently, more powerful queries can be written, and management of complex information systems can be performed more effectively. However, security of complex information systems should also be considered besides these advantages of OBDA. Ontology Based Access Control (OBAC) enables the enforcement of an access control mechanism through the utilization of Semantic Web technologies. Thus, only authorized entities can access and modify data. In this study, the OBAC and OBDA approaches are integrated. The proposed Semantic Web based solution's goal is to ensure data security and preserve privacy while providing an efficient processing of data from different heterogeneous sources.

Keywords: Data security · Privacy · Access control · Data access · Semantic web · Ontology

1 Introduction

The recent advancements in modern technology have led to a significant increase in data growth. Furthermore, this massive amount of data is constantly growing as data continues to flow in from various sources such as sensors, Internet of Things (IoT) devices, and so on. As a result of this rapid growth, there are several data sources that require data integration. Moreover, analyzing and evaluating this big data is essential for obtaining meaningful query results and accessing meaningful information. Further, data integration is required for effective data utilization [1]. However, the great majority of these data is published in formats that are not directly processes by the analytical tools

Supported by Ege University Scientific Research Projects Committee under the grant number 18-MUH-036.

[2]. The integration problem of different data sources is eliminated by storing the data in ontologies [3]. An ontology is a semantic data schema paradigm and defined as *a formal, explicit specification of a shared conceptualization* [4]. An ontology represents concepts and relationships between these concepts that are used to describe a domain. Thus, ontologies provide a high-level global schema of data sources and a vocabulary for user queries [5].

Ontology Based Data Access (OBDA) is a semantic data integration approach that allows to access data stored in the existing data sources. Therefore, the OBDA approach allows to conceptually specify the data and enables to abstract the technical-schema-level details of the data. OBDA follows the Global-as-View (GaV) approach and represents a unified global view over different data sources. For this purpose, a global ontology is built as a metadata representation of the data elements and their relationships, and the semantic mappings between the global ontology and the data sources are established [6]. Semantic mapping is the process that the relevant entities in the database are linked with the concepts of ontology. The semantic mapping between an ontology and a database is recognized as a case of data integration [7]. Thereby, the mapping between ontology concepts and legacy relational data enables the retrieval of more enriched query results and supports more effective data analytics.

OBDA supports the decision-making systems by enabling flexible and effective information sharing between multiple systems. For this purpose, OBDA presents a conceptual representation of a domain and achieves data virtualization. Data virtualization integrates data without moving and transforming them [8]. Data virtualization creates a centralized point of access while introducing security requirements including privacy, access control, authentication, authorization, and data integrity. Therefore, effective mechanisms are needed to ensure the data security and preserve privacy.

Ontology Based Access Control (OBAC) provides a Semantic Web-based access control mechanism for the security requirements. For this purpose, OBAC enables to create, modify and query semantically-rich policies over domain knowledge [9–11]. Therefore, access to information is only achieved by authorized entities. Hence, OBAC provides a semantic-aware solution for the security requirements of OBDA.

In this study, OBAC and OBDA are integrated to provide a data model-independent access control. The goal of this integration is to ensure data security and preserve privacy while also providing the efficient processing of data from various heterogeneous data sources. For this goal, the OBAC model is enhanced with the OBDA paradigm. Therefore, semantic access to data sources is achieved and unauthorized access requests are prevented. As a result, data virtualization is provided while ensuring security and preserving privacy.

This study is an extended version of the previous work presented in [12]. In this study, the conceptual model proposed in [12] is established. For this purpose, a use case study for the healthcare domain is presented. Therefore, Hospital Database, Hospital Ontology and Hospital Policy Ontology are created and mappings are established. Further, various queries are performed on the hospital data. Moreover, the proposed model is implemented for the healthcare domain.

The organization of the paper is as follows: Sect. 2 reviews the related work, Sect. 3 clarifies the proposed solution to ensure data security and preserve privacy for OBDA, Sect. 4 presents a use case of the proposed solution for the healthcare domain. Finally, Sect. 5 concludes and summarizes the future work.

2   Related Work

In today's technological environment, being data-driven is essential for staying competitive, creating innovation, and making better decisions based on information and analysis. Thus, data should be integrated to be effectively used by decision-making systems. For this purpose, data integration requires cleaning, de-duplicating, and homogenizing the data coming from diverse sources [8]. However, data integration is a difficult task as most data sources are heterogeneous and data are published in formats that cannot be processed directly by analytic tools [7, 13]. Therefore, databases are mapped to ontology representations to access the existing data sources in an efficient and flexible way. An ontology allows information to be represented in a machine-readable form. Therefore, information can be reused, shared, and used to make deductions.

The relationship between the Semantic Web and the relational databases is studied in [14]. For this purpose, a methodology is adopted and an understanding on practicing the data integration by using relational databases and Semantic Web technologies is presented. The steps for transforming relational databases to ontology representation are described in [7]. The study also presents the mapping tools, the requirements of the mapping tools, their benefits and drawbacks. A similar approach presented in [15] also transforms relational database to an ontology and proposes an approach for a direct mapping to mine semantic information from data sources. A survey that reviews tools, methods, and applications for the integration of relational databases into the Semantic Web is presented in [16].

The mappings are used to establish the relationship between the Semantic Web and the relational databases. OBDA is a prevalent approach for creating a mapping between a database and an ontology. As a result, it simplifies the data access process and improves the quality of query results. Therefore, OBDA is considered as a crucial component of the new generation of information systems [5]. In the literature, OBDA is used for dealing with huge amounts of heterogeneous data in various domains. For instance, data access challenges in a petroleum company [17], energy technology database within the technology forecasting information system [18], end-user access to industrial Big Data stores [19], semantically integrating manufacturing data to support product quality analysis [1], and ontology-based semantic access to biological data [20]. Further, OBDA based approaches are implemented to bind the farming data sources with various external datasets for the agriculture domain [21], to enable the access to cultural and historical data about commercial trade system and food production during the Roman Empire [22], and to combine and process static and real-time data from multiple sources in the maritime security domain [23]. Regarding the studies presented in the literature, an effective data visualization and sharing of information among multiple data sources is achieved by OBDA.

Data virtualization provides a centralized point of access. Hence, data should be protected against unauthorized access. Therefore, effective mechanisms are needed to meet the security requirements. In Semantic Web, access control is a challenging issue and access to resources should be controlled. For this purpose, ontology based access control mechanisms are developed. A policy language and a security framework to address security requirements in Semantic Web are presented [24,25]. In [26], a Role-Based Access Control (RBAC) model is extended to implement an access control mechanism for Semantic Web services. A Semantic Based Access Control model (SBAC) is presented in [27] to authenticate users based on their credentials when requesting an access right. An Ontology Based Access Control (OBAC) model is proposed in [9–11] to define and enforce semantically rich access control policies. The domain-independent OBAC uses the Rei policy language [24] to model both the requestor and the requested source. Further, an ontological access control approach is applied for various domains, such as the healthcare domain [28], online social networks and cloud computing [29].

The main motivation of this study is integrating OBAC model with the concepts of OBDA to improve security and to preserve privacy while providing data virtualization. The main contribution of this study is providing a data model-independent access control. Therefore, access to data sources is abstracted independent of the underlying mapping. To the best of our knowledge, the proposed study presents a novel and the first approach for enhancing security and preserving privacy for the OBDA paradigm.

3   Data Model-Independent Access Control

Data integration enables to manipulate data transparently across various data sources [30]. As most of the data sources are heterogeneous, providing data integration becomes a difficult task [7]. Moreover, providing the semantics of the stored data is essential. Therefore, semantic data integration enables the use of the conceptual representation of data and their relationships. Therefore, it eliminates the possible heterogeneities [30]. Further, Semantic Web provides reasoning, dynamic schema, graph traversal, variable predicate, and data integration for integrating relational databases with the Semantic Web technologies [14].

OBDA allows querying a database that uses an ontology to expose data by abstracting away from the technical schema-level details of the underlying data [19]. OBDA is based on three main components: ontology, data source, and mapping. The structure of OBDA is given in Fig. 1. Ontology provides a unified and conceptual view of the data, data source is the external and independent repositories (possibly multiple and heterogeneous), and mapping associates data resources with the concepts of the ontology.

In OBDA, domain knowledge is represented in the form of an ontology, and data virtualization is achieved through a mapping between the data sources and the domain ontology [34]. When the desired mapping is established, the user can execute queries on the ontology and retrieve data from the mapped database [16]. Thus, a conceptual view of data is presented with OBDA. Besides, the ontology acts as a mediator between the user and the data. In this work, the OBAC model is integrated within the scope of the OBDA approach. OBAC is an access control mechanism that is used to secure Semantic Web based applications. The aim of integrating the OBAC model within the scope of OBDA is to provide a privacy framework. Thus, an ontology-based data access can be performed in a privacy-aware manner. Hence, an access control mechanism will be

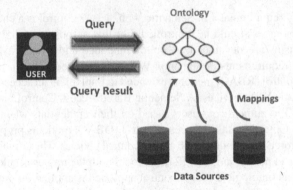

Fig. 1. The structure of OBDA.

enforced for the OBDA, and security-enhanced and privacy-aware OBDA based on the OBAC model will be achieved. Moreover, access control needs to be managed on different data models due to polyglot persistence. As the legacy data can be represented in an ontology, relational database, or non-relational database, queries should be translated into a form that will be understood by the legacy data. This process will be achieved by mapping. The overall architecture of the proposed model is given in Fig. 2 [12]. The proposed model enforces the access control mechanism for the OBDA.

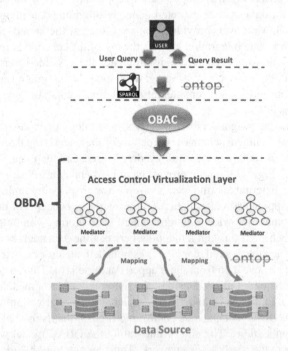

Fig. 2. The architecture of the proposed model [12].

The proposed model is based on a materialization-based approach (forward chaining). In the materialization-base approach [14], the input is the database D, the target ontology is O and the mapping from D to O is M. The legacy data source is the ABox (A) and the ontology is the TBox (T). The SPARQL [31] query Q is executed over the D, O, and M. The OBAC model is based on Rei policy ontologies [24,25]. The mapping between a database and an ontology is achieved by Ontop [32] which is an open-source OBDA framework. Also, Ontop is a query transformation module. Thus, queries are executed by utilizing the Ontop framework.

In OBDA, data sources are accessed through a conceptual layer. The related conceptual layer is a RDF or an OWL ontology and uses R2RML mappings to connect to the underlying database. R2RML is a language that expresses customized mappings from relational databases to RDF datasets [33]. R2RML generates the RDF triple from the relational database based on the mapping. For this purpose, R2RML specifies a mapping that refers to a logical table to retrieve data from the input database and the logical table maps to Triples Maps. The logical table that is taken as an input corresponds to a database table, a database view, or SQL query. The mappings are written in Turtle syntax. Hence, the structure of the relational database is reflected by the RDF graph.

Consequently, the related ontology can be queried with SPARQL. Thus, OBDA retrieves the elements from the data sources and uses the related mappings to generate the query answers. However, access to information should be achieved by authorized entities. For this purpose, OBAC model is integrated with OBDA. This integration allows enhancing data security and improving privacy while providing an efficient processing of data from multiple heterogeneous sources.

The main elements of an access control mechanism are the subject, object and access right. The subject is the entity that requests access to an object, the object is the source to be accessed, and the access right specifies the way in which a subject may access an object. Subjects access resources to perform an action for a specific purpose and an action is the operation that is performed on the source by the subject. In order to provide the fully semantic representation of data that is aimed by the Semantic Web, the elements within the access control mechanism must also be semantically represented. OBAC [9–11] aims to provide the desired semantics for the access control mechanism. For this purpose, the subject that requests an access, the object to be accessed, the actions that can be performed on this object, and the constraints that specify the conditions under which these actions can be performed are defined in OBAC. Moreover, OBAC provides a domain-independent access control. Thus, OBAC can be applied in various domains. OBAC is based on Rei policy language [24,25] and allows to create, modify, and delete policies. Policies can specified as permissions, prohibitions, obligations, and dispensations. Permission states what an entity can do, Prohibition specifies what an entity can't do, Obligation denotes what an entity should do, and Dispensation indicates what an entity need no longer do.

The novelty aspects of the proposed model are as follows: (i) establishing an integrated framework model to achieve data access, preserve privacy and ensure access control, (ii) realization of a data model-independent access control mechanism, (iii) execution of queries in both reactive and proactive structure, and (iv) providing a privacy-aware OBDA model.

4   A Use Case for Healthcare Domain

In this study, the healthcare domain is chosen as the application domain to realize the security enhanced and privacy aware OBDA approach. For this purpose, first, a hospital database is created, then a hospital ontology and a hospital policy ontology based on the hospital ontology are created. Ontologies are created with Protégé ontology editor [35]. After creating the related ontologies, the mapping between the hospital database and ontologies are established by utilizing the Ontop framework [32]. Finally, various queries are executed by using Ontop SPARQL.

4.1   Hospital Database

The hospital database is created by using the MySQL database management system [36]. The created tables shown in Fig. 3 are as follows: `action`, `appointments`, `basicscience`, `bloodtests`, `departments`, `doctor`, `doctorpatient`, `equipments`, `granting`, `invoice`, `laboratory`, `laboratorytechnician`, `mechanicaltechnician`, `medicalscience`, `medicalstudent`, `nurse`, `officer`, `patient`, `permission`, `prescriptions`, `prohibition`, `radiologytechnician`, `room`, `surgicalscience`. Further, sample data are inserted into tables as shown in Fig. 4.

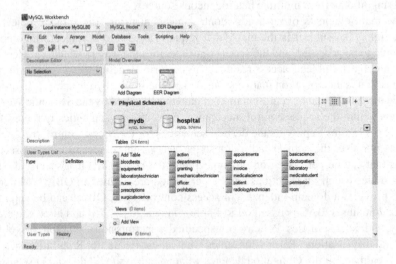

Fig. 3. Tables of Hospital Database.

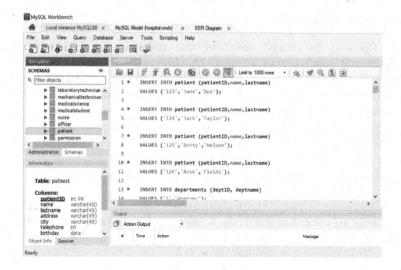

Fig. 4. Inserting records in tables.

The contents of the created tables are as follows:

- Action: Specifies the related actions that can be performed on data.
- Appointments: Indicates patients' doctor appointments.
- Basicscience: The Basic Sciences department of the hospital.
- Bloodtests: Results of blood tests performed in the hospital.
- Departments: Indicates the departments in the hospital.
- Doctor: Indicates doctors working in the hospital.
- Doctorpatient: Indicates the doctor-patient relationship.
- Equipments: Indicates the technical devices in the hospital.
- Granting: Indicates the approved hospital policies.
- Invoice: Indicates hospital bills listing the charges of patient visits.
- Laboratory: Indicates the laboratories in the hospital.
- Laboratorytechnician: Indicates technicians working in the hospital laboratories.
- Mechanicaltechnician: Indicates the mechanical technicians working in the hospital.
- Medicalscience: The Medical Sciences department of the hospital.
- Medicalstudent: Indicates the medical students working in the hospital.
- Nurse: Indicates the nurses working in the hospital.
- Officer: Indicates the office workers in the hospital.
- Patient: Specifies the patient information.
- Permission: Specifies the actions that are allowed.
- Prescriptions: Indicates prescriptions written to the patients.
- Prohibition: Specifies the actions that are not allowed.
- Radiologytechnician: Specifies radiology technicians working in the hospital laboratories.
- Room: Indicates the patient rooms in the hospital.
- Surgicalscience: The Surgical Sciences department of the hospital.

4.2 Hospital Ontology

Hospital Ontology is created based on the tables in the Hospital Database. The classes and subclasses of Hospital Ontology are as follows: `Acounting`, `Administration`, `Appointments`, `Departments`, `BasicScience`, `MedicalScience`, `SurgicalScience`, `Documents`, `HealthReports`, `Prescriptions`, `Results`, `BloodTests`, `RadiologyResults`, `CAT`, `CT`, `Mammography`, `MRA`, `MRI`, `PET`, `XRay`, `UrineTests`, `VaccinationCard`, `Equipments`, `Laboratory`, `Patient`, `Room`, `Staff`, `Doctor`, `Intern`, `MedicalStudent`, `Nurse`, `Officer`, `Technician`, `LaboratoryTechnician`, `MechanicalTechnician`, `RadiologyTechnician`, `UltrasoundTechnician`. Further, object and data type properties are created to specify the relationship between concepts and their internal structure. The ontology metrics of the Hospital Ontology are shown in the Fig. 5.

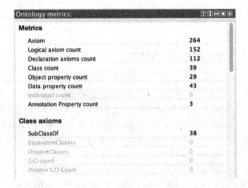

Fig. 5. The ontology metrics of the Hospital Ontology.

4.3 Hospital Policy Ontology

Hospital Policy Ontology is created based on the OBAC model [10] and Rei policy ontology [24]. Hospital Policy Ontology is an access control policy that aims to achieve the security and privacy requirements of the organization. Thus, the policy ontology uses the Hospital Ontology as the domain ontology. The Hospital Policy Ontology's class hierarchy is shown in Fig. 6.

As shown in the class hierarchy of Hospital Policy Ontology, actions that can be performed on hospital data are represented in the `Action` class. The actions added to the `Action` class are as follows: `CreatingInvoice`, `DeletingInvoice`, `EditingDocuments`, `EditingInvoice`, `EditingResults`, `EditVaccinationCalendar`, `ViewPrescription`, `ViewResults`, `ViewVaccinationCalendar`, and `WritingPrescription`. In the Hospital Policy Ontology, there are also `Policy`, `Permission`, `Prohibition`,

Fig. 6. The Hospital Policy Ontology's class hierarchy.

Granting, and SimpleConstraint classes to specify the rights to access and actions that can be performed on the hospital data. Figure 7 shows the ontology metrics of the Hospital Policy Ontology.

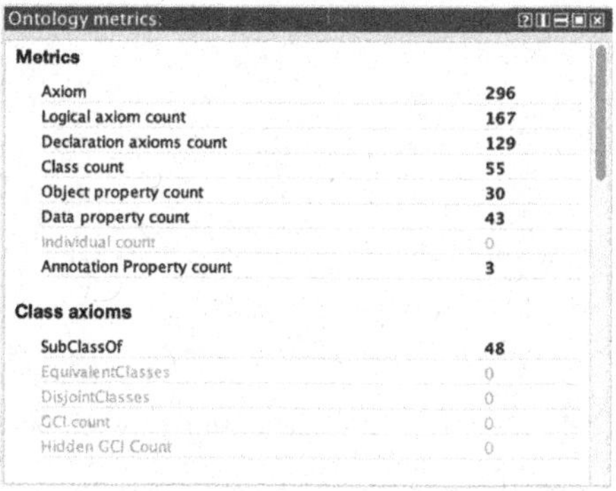

Fig. 7. The Hospital Policy Ontology's metrics.

4.4   Mappings Between the Database and Ontology

The mappings between the Hospital Database and the Hospital Policy Ontology are established after creating the Hospital Policy Ontology. Ontop framework [32] is used to establish the mappings. Therefore, the mappings between tables of the Hospital Database and classes of the Hospital Ontology are established.

After creating the mappings between tables in the database and classes in the policy ontology, the mappings for the relationships between concepts are established. An example mapping for the relationship between a Doctor and a Patient is shown in Fig. 8. The mapping shown in Fig. 8 indicates that the relationship between the Doctor and the Patient class is defined with hasPatient property in the target Hospital Ontology. Further, the database query regarding the relevant Doctor-Patient relationship is specified in the source (SQL query) field of the mapping. Finally, the third section of the mapping shows the query results obtained from the execution of this SQL query.

Fig. 8. The mapping for the hasPatient relationship between Doctor and Patient.

Finally, the mappings for the Permission and Prohibition to control access to hospital data are established as shown in Fig. 9 and Fig. 10, respectively. These mappings represent the actions that are allowed or prohibited. For example, in Fig. 9, the doctor "Miranda Bailey" has permission to read the blood test results of the patient "Jane Doe", but does not have the right to make changes in the blood test results according to the prohibitions presented in Fig. 10.

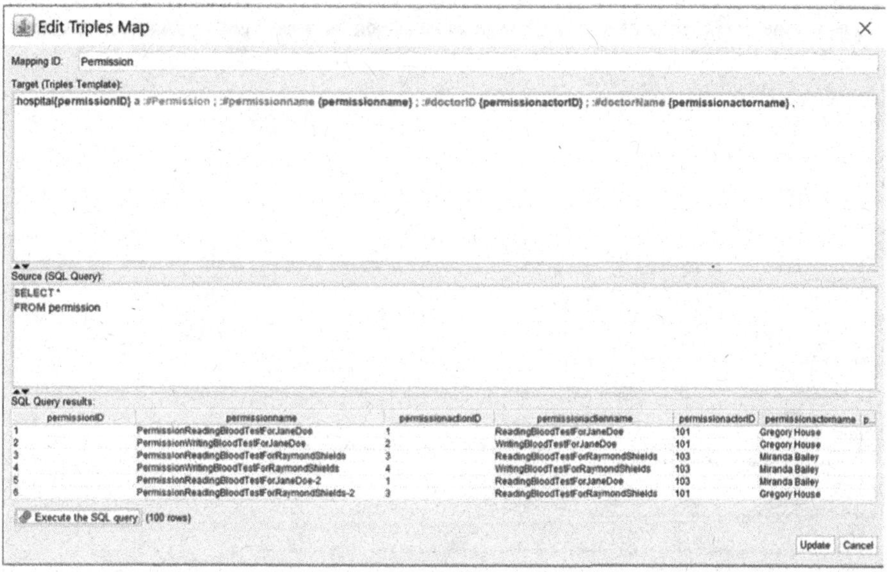

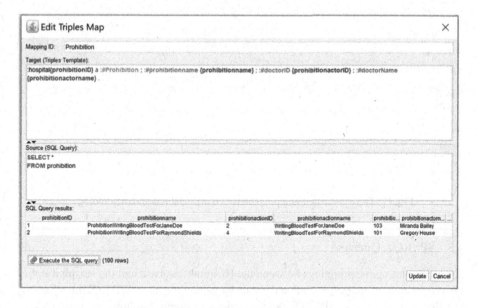

Fig. 9. The mapping for `Permission`.

Fig. 10. The mapping for `Prohibition`.

Similarly, all the related mappings are established between the Hospital Database and the Hospital Policy Ontology. The final mapping table is presented in Fig. 11.

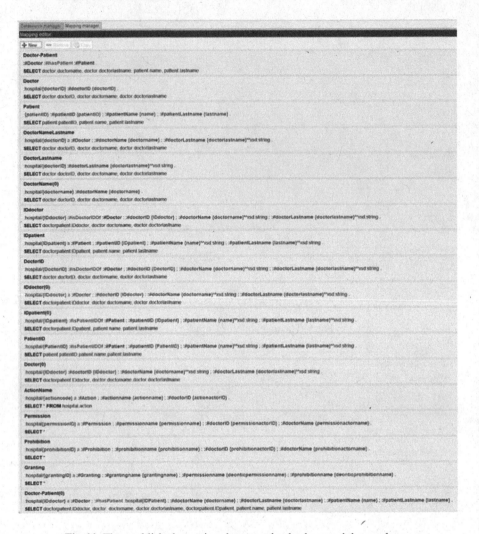

Fig. 11. The established mappings between the database and the ontology.

4.5 SPARQL Queries

After completing the mappings between the Hospital Database and the Hospital Policy Ontology, queries are performed on the data by using the Ontop SPARQL query editor. For this purpose, Ontop SPARQL Manager is used. Figure 12 shows the query results of patients' doctors in the database. The goal of the related query is listing the relationship between doctors and their patients. Therefore, the listed results represent the hasPatient relationship between the Doctor and the Patient shown in Fig. 8. The query results show the doctorID, doctorname, doctorlastname, patientID, patientname, and patientlastname.

Fig. 12. The SPARQL query results for the patients' doctors.

The permission and prohibition policies to enforce the access rights to ensure security and privacy are also queried. In this context, the SPARQL query results regarding the permissions and prohibitions defined in the system are presented in Fig. 13 and Fig. 14, respectively. The query results in Fig. 13 shows access permissions defined for doctors in the system. Thereupon, permissions, the IDs and names of actors who are permitted to perform the related action are listed. The actions that can not be performed on data are shown in Fig. 14.

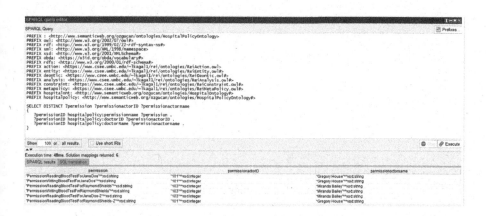

Fig. 13. The SPARQL query results for the defined Permissions.

Finally, the proposed model is implemented with Apache Jena Framework [37]. Apache Jena is an open source framework to build Semantic Web based applications.

Figure 15 shows the definition of permission and prohibition policies. As seen, policies are defined by specifying `Policy Type`, `Policy Name`, `Actor`, `Action`, `Constraint`, and `Description`. `Policy Type` is the policy deontic object that allows to create permissions, prohibitions, obligations and dispensations

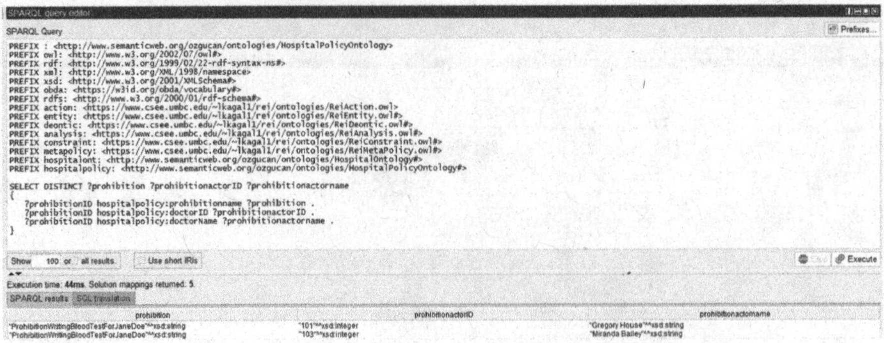

Fig. 14. The SPARQL query results for the defined Prohibitions.

over entities in the domain. `Policy Name` feature is the name of the defined policy to clearly state the policy's goal. `Actor` is the subject who requests to access to a resource and `Action` indicates the action that the `Actor` requests to perform. `Constraint` specifies the constraint under which the policy will be executed. The `Constraint` defines the resource that the `Actor` requests to access. Finally, the `Description` is used to specify the related policy's description. The defined Permission and Prohibition policies are shown in Fig. 16 and Fig. 17, respectively.

Fig. 15. The policy definition.

The ontological representation of `PermissionReadingBloodTestForJane Doe` and `ProhibitionWritingBloodTestForJaneDoe` are as follows:

```
<policy:deontic>
    <deontic:Permission rdf:ID="PermissionReadingBloodTestForJaneDoe">
        <policy:desc rdf:datatype="http://www.w3.org/2001/XMLSchema#string">
            Gregory House can read Jane Doe's blood test results.
        </policy:desc>
        <deontic:action rdf:resource="#ReadingBloodTestForJaneDoe"/>
        <deontic:actor rdf:resource="#GregoryHouse"/>
        <deontic:constraint rdf:resource="#BloodTest_JaneDoe"/>
```

```
    </deontic:Permission>
  </policy:deontic>


  <policy:deontic>
    <deontic:Prohibition rdf:ID="ProhibitionWritingBloodTestForJaneDoe">
      <policy:desc rdf:datatype="http://www.w3.org/2001/XMLSchema#string">
        Miranda Bailey can't write to Jane Doe's blood test
        results.
      </policy:desc>
      <deontic:action rdf:resource="#WritingBloodTestForJaneDoe"/>
      <deontic:actor rdf:resource="#MirandaBailey"/>
      <deontic:constraint rdf:resource="#BloodTest_JaneDoe"/>
    </deontic:Prohibition>
  </policy:deontic>
```

Hospital   Home Privacy

Policy ID	Policy Type	Policy Name	Policy Actor	Policy Action	Policy Constraint	Policy Description		
1	Permission	PermissionReadingBloodTestForJaneDoe	Gregory House	ReadingBloodTestForJaneDoe	BloodTest_JaneDoe	Gregory House can read Jane Doe's blood test results.	Update	Delete
2	Permission	PermissionWritingBloodTestForJaneDoe	Gregory House	WritingBloodTestForJaneDoe	BloodTest_JaneDoe	Gregory House can write Jane Doe's blood test results.	Update	Delete
3	Permission	PermissionReadingBloodTestForRaymondShields	Miranda Bailey	ReadingBloodTestForRaymondShields	BloodTest_RaymondShields	Miranda Bailey can read Raymond Shields's blood test results.	Update	Delete
4	Permission	PermissionWritingBloodTestForRaymondShields	Miranda Bailey	WritingBloodTestForRaymondShields	BloodTest_RaymondShields	Miranda Bailey can write Raymond Shields's blood test results.	Update	Delete
5	Permission	PermissionReadingBloodTestForJaneDoe-2	Miranda Bailey	ReadingBloodTestForJaneDoe	BloodTest_JaneDoe	Miranda Bailey can read Jane Doe's blood test results.	Update	Delete
6	Permission	PermissionReadingBloodTestForRaymondShields-2	Gregory House	ReadingBloodTestForRaymondShields	BloodTest_RaymondShields	Gregory House can read Raymond Shields's blood test results.	Update	Delete

Fig. 16. The list of Permission policies.

As a result, OBAC and OBDA approaches are integrated to provide a data model-independent access control. This integration enables to abstract access to data sources independent of the underlying mapping. Therefore, data security is ensured and patient's privacy is preserved. Meanwhile, an efficient processing of data that exists in different data sources is provided.

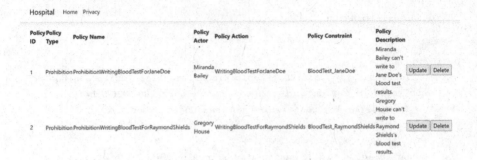

Fig. 17. The list of Prohibition policies.

5   Conclusions and Future Work

The majority of daily routines in today's world rely on information systems and these data are generally stored in the relational databases. The database requires to be converted to the knowledge base to extract semantic information from the database, inference it and obtain valuable information [38]. Therefore, the mapping between databases and ontologies should be maintained to execute semantic queries and to discover new relationships by inference. Consequently, the quality of the data integration will be improved. However, the security and privacy of systems must also be maintained. In this study, a Semantic Web based model is proposed to improve the security and privacy of systems that may arise when applying the OBDA approach. The proposed study is based on the conceptual model presented in [12]. The main goal of this study is to develop a security enhanced and privacy-aware OBDA solution while abstracting access to data sources independent of the underlying mapping. Therefore, OBAC and OBDA approaches are integrated and a use case study is presented for the hospital domain.

As a future work, RBAC mechanism will be integrated into the model. In the RBAC model, permissions are given directly to roles, not to the user. For this purpose, a query on a relational database should be transformed from RBAC to OBAC. Thus, each data source will be queried in its environment. Therefore, the RBAC model will be mapped to the OBAC model where data is represented semantically and the conversion of RBAC entities to OBAC entities for relational data sources will be achieved.

Acknowledgements. This study is supported by Ege University Scientific Research Projects Committee under the grant number 18-MUH-036.

References

1. Kalaycı, E.G., Grangel González, I., Lösch, F., Xiao, G., ul-Mehdi, A., Kharlamov, E., Calvanese, D.: Semantic integration of bosch manufacturing data using virtual knowledge graphs. In: Pan, J.Z., Tamma, V., d'Amato, C., Janowicz, K., Fu, B., Polleres, A., Seneviratne, O., Kagal, L. (eds.) ISWC 2020. LNCS, vol. 12507, pp. 464–481. Springer, Cham (2020). https://doi.org/10.1007/978-3-030-62466-8_29

2. Touma, R., Romero, O., Jovanovic, P.: Supporting data integration tasks with semi-automatic ontology construction. In: Proceedings of the ACM Eighteenth International Workshop on Data Warehousing and OLAP (DOLAP'15), pp. 89–98. (2015). https://doi.org/10.1145/2811222.2811228
3. Can, O., Sezer, E., Bursa, O., Unalir, M.O.: Comparing relational and ontological triple stores in healthcare domain. Entropy **19**(1), 30 (2017)
4. Gruber, T.-R.: Towards principles for the design of ontologies used for knowledge sharing. Int. J. Hum Comput. Stud. **43**(5–6), 907–928 (1995)
5. Kontchakov, R., Rodríguez-Muro, M., Zakharyaschev, M.: Ontology-based data access with databases: a short course. In: Rudolph, S., Gottlob, G., Horrocks, I., van Harmelen, F. (eds.) Reasoning Web 2013. LNCS, vol. 8067, pp. 194–229. Springer, Heidelberg (2013). https://doi.org/10.1007/978-3-642-39784-4_5
6. Zhang, H., Guo, Y., Li, Q., George, T.J., Shenkman, E.A., Bian, J.: Data integration through ontology-based data access to support integrative data analysis: a case study of cancer survival. In: IEEE International Conference on Bioinformatics and Biomedicine (BIBM), pp. 1300–1303. (2017). https://doi.org/10.1109/BIBM.2017.8217849
7. Haw, S.-C., May, J.-W., Subramaniam, S.: Mapping relational databases to ontology representation: a review. In: Proceedings of the International Conference on Digital Technology in Education (ICDTE'17), pp. 54–55. (2017). https://doi.org/10.1145/3134847.3134852
8. Xiao, G., Ding, L., Cogrel, B., Calvanese, D.: Virtual knowledge graphs: an overview of systems and use cases. Data Intell. **1**(3), 201–223 (2019)
9. Can, O.: Personalizable Ontology Based Access Control for Semantic Web and Policy Management. Ph.D. thesis, Ege University, Department of Computer Engineering. (2009)
10. Can, O., Bursa, O., Unalir, M.O.: Personalizable ontology based access control. Gazi Univ. J. Sci. **23**(4), 465–474 (2010)
11. Can, O., Unalir, M.O.: Ontology based access control. Pamukkale Univ. J. Eng. Sci. **16**(2), 197–206 (2010)
12. Can, O., Unalir, M.O.: Revisiting ontology based access control: the case for ontology based data access. In: Proceedings of the 8th International Conference on Information Systems Security and Privacy (ICISSP 2022), pp. 515–518 (2022)
13. Bishr, Y.A.: Overcoming the semantic and other barriers to GIS interoperability. Int. J. Geogr. Inf. Sci. **12**(4), 229–314 (1998)
14. Sequeda, J.F.: Integrating relational databases with the semantic web: a reflection. In: Ianni, G., Lembo, D., Bertossi, L., Faber, W., Glimm, B., Gottlob, G., Staab, S. (eds.) Reasoning Web 2017. LNCS, vol. 10370, pp. 68–120. Springer, Cham (2017). https://doi.org/10.1007/978-3-319-61033-7_4
15. Hazber, M.A.G., Li, R., Gu, X., Xu, G.: Integration mapping rules: transforming relational database to semantic web ontology. Appl. Math. Inf. Sci. **10**(3), 881–901 (2016)
16. Spanos, D.E., Stavrou, P., Mitrou, N.: Bringing relational databases into the semantic web: a survey. Semantic Web **3**(2), 169–209 (2012)
17. Kharlamov, E., Hovland, D., Jimenez-Rui, E., et al.: Ontology based data access in statoil. J. Web Semant. **44**, 3–36 (2017)
18. Mikheev, A.V.: Ontology-based data access for energy technology forecasting. In: Proceedings of the 5th International workshop on Critical infrastructures: Contingency management, Intelligent, Agent-based, Cloud computing and Cyber security (IWCI 2018), Advances in Intelligent Systems Research, Volume 158, pp. 147–151. (2018). https://doi.org/10.2991/iwci-18.2018.26

19. Kharlamov, E., Jiménez-Ruiz, E., Zheleznyakov, D., Bilidas, D., Giese, M., Haase, P., Horrocks, I., Kllapi, H., Koubarakis, M., Özçep, Ö., Rodríguez-Muro, M., Rosati, R., Schmidt, M., Schlatte, R., Soylu, A., Waaler, A.: Optique: towards OBDA systems for industry. In: Cimiano, P., Fernández, M., Lopez, V., Schlobach, S., Völker, J. (eds.) ESWC 2013. LNCS, vol. 7955, pp. 125–140. Springer, Heidelberg (2013). https://doi.org/10.1007/978-3-642-41242-4_11

20. Hoehndorf, R., Slater, L., Schofield, P.-N., et al.: Aber-owl: a framework for ontology-based data access in biology. BMC Bioinformatics 16(26) (2015)

21. Pokharel, S., Sherif, M.A., Lehmann, J.: Ontology based data access and integration for improving the effectiveness of farming in Nepal. In: 2014 IEEE/WIC/ACM International Joint Conferences on Web Intelligence (WI) and Intelligent Agent Technologies (IAT), pp. 319–326. (2014). https://doi.org/10.1109/WI-IAT.2014.114

22. Calvanese, D., et al.: Ontology-based data integration in EPNet: production and distribution of food during the Roman Empire. Eng. Appl. Artif. Intell. 51, 212–229 (2016)

23. Brüggemann, S., Bereta, K., Xiao, G., Koubarakis, M.: Ontology-based data access for maritime security. In: Sack, H., Blomqvist, E., d'Aquin, M., Ghidini, C., Ponzetto, S.P., Lange, C. (eds.) ESWC 2016. LNCS, vol. 9678, pp. 741–757. Springer, Cham (2016). https://doi.org/10.1007/978-3-319-34129-3_45

24. Kagal, L.: Rei: A Policy Language for the Me-Centric Project. HP Laboratories Palo Alto (2002)

25. Kagal, L., Finin, T., Joshi, A.: A policy based approach to security for the semantic web. In: Fensel, D., Sycara, K., Mylopoulos, J. (eds.) ISWC 2003. LNCS, vol. 2870, pp. 402–418. Springer, Heidelberg (2003). https://doi.org/10.1007/978-3-540-39718-2_26

26. He, Z., Huang, K., Wu, L., Li, H., Lai, H.: Using semantic web techniques to implement access control for web service. In: Zhu, R., Zhang, Y., Liu, B., Liu, C. (eds.) ICICA 2010. CCIS, vol. 105, pp. 258–266. Springer, Heidelberg (2010). https://doi.org/10.1007/978-3-642-16336-4_34

27. Javanmardi, S., Amini, M., Jalili, R.: An access control model for protecting semantic web resources. In: Proceedings of the ISWC'06 Workshop on Semantic Web Policy (SWPW'06) (2006)

28. Mohan, K., Aramudhan, M.: Ontology based access control model for healthcare system in cloud computing. Indian J. Sci. Technol. 8(S9), 213–217 (2015)

29. Imran-Daud, M., Sanchez, D., Viejo, A.: Ontology-based access control management: two use cases. In: Proceedings of the 8th International Conference on Agents and Artificial Intelligence (ICAART), vol. 1, pp. 244–249 (2016). https://doi.org/0.5220/0005777902440249

30. Cruz, I.F., Xiao, H.: The role of ontologies in data integration. Int. J. Eng. Intell. Syst. Electr. Eng. Commun. 13(4), 245–252 (2005)

31. W3C Recommendation: SPARQL Query Language for RDF (2008). https://www.w3.org/TR/rdf-sparqlquery. Accessed 24 Nov 2022

32. Ontop Framework. https://ontop-vkg.org. Accessed 24 Nov 2022

33. Das, S., Sundara, S., Cyganiak, R.: R2RML: RDB to RDF Mapping Language (2012). https://www.w3.org/TR/r2rml/. Accessed 24 Nov 2022

34. Poggi, A., Lembo, D., Calvanese, D., De Giacomo, G., Lenzerini, M., Rosati, R.: Linking data to ontologies. In: Spaccapietra, S. (ed.) Journal on Data Semantics X. LNCS, vol. 4900, pp. 133–173. Springer, Heidelberg (2008). https://doi.org/10.1007/978-3-540-77688-8_5

35. Protégé Ontology Editor. https://protege.stanford.edu. Accessed 24 Nov 2022

36. MySQL. https://www.mysql.com. Accessed 24 Nov 2022

37. Apache Jena Framework. https://jena.apache.org. Accessed 24 Nov 2022

38. Dadjoo, M., Kheirkhah, E.: An approach for transforming of relational databases to owl ontology. Int. J. Web Semant. Technol. 6(1), 19–28 (2015)

Experimentally Obtained Differential-Linear Distinguishers for Permutations of ASCON and DryGASCON

Aslı Başak Civek◉ and Cihangir Tezcan(✉)◉

Graduate School of Informatics, Department of Cyber Security, Middle East Technical
University, Ankara, Turkey
{abcivek,cihangir}@metu.edu.tr

Abstract. DRYGASCON and ASCON are two similar authenticated encryption
algorithms submitted to NIST's recently finalized lightweight cryptography competition. DRYGASCON was eliminated after the second round, while ASCON
won the competition and became the new lightweight cryptography standard.
We analyze these two ciphers using differential-linear distinguishers to better
understand their security. By using the parallel computing power of GPUs, we
show that better distinguishers can be obtained experimentally in practice which
cannot be obtained theoretically by known methods. We offer the best experimentally obtained 5-round differential-linear distinguishers for the permutations
of ASCON and DRYGASCON. We also provide related-key differential-linear
attacks on 5-round ASCON.

Keywords: Lightweight cryptography · Cryptanalysis · Differential-linear ·
NIST

1 Introduction

Advanced Encryption Standard (AES) [9] is arguably the most used encryption algorithm in the world and after more than 20 years of cryptanalysis effort, it is still secure
against known attack techniques. Although AES is secure and suitable for many platforms, many companies chose to implement proprietary ciphers in their hardware when
new technologies required resource-constrained devices. The total break of these proprietary algorithms resulted in many disasters, like the cloning of smartcards [19] or
unauthorized access to cars [13]. That is why NIST launched a competition to select one
or more lightweight standards [18] for resource-constrained devices that cannot effectively use the existing ones. The competition, which started in April 2019, received
57 applications. NIST accepted 56 of them in the first round. As a result of analyses
by the crypto community, 32 algorithms remained in Round 2 in August 2019, with
ASCON and DRYGASCON being two of them. In March 2021, 10 algorithms made it

The work of Cihangir Tezcan has been supported by TUBITAK 1001 Project under the grant
number 121E228 and by Middle East Technical University Scientific Research Projects Coordi-
nation Unit under grant number AGEP-704-2023-11294.

P. Mori et al. (Eds.): ICISSP 2021/ICISSP 2022, CCIS 1851, pp. 91–103, 2023.
https://doi.org/10.1007/978-3-031-37807-2_5

to the finals, with Ascon ultimately winning the competition on February 7, 2023 [20]. Before the competition, NIST had three symmetric encryption standards: AES, 3DES, and SKIPJACK. SKIPJACK only supports 80-bit secret key which is not long enough to withstand exhaustive key search attacks. Thus, SKIPJACK is allowed only for legacy use. Moreover, NIST's support for 3DES will end in 2024. Thus, the addition of ASCON to NIST's symmetric encryption standards would provide an alternative to AES when AES is not preferable in certain scenarios.

Security was one of the most important criteria in the Lightweight Cryptography Competition and the cryptanalysis effort of the cryptography community during the competition was vital for NIST's selection process. Many cryptanalysis technique starts with a statistical observation called a distinguisher. A distinguisher is a property that is observed with different probabilities for a random permutation and a part of a cipher. Thus, a distinguisher is used to distinguish a part of the cipher from a random permutation and every attack starts with a distinguisher. Linear cryptanalysis [17] and differential cryptanalysis [6] are the most studied cryptanalysis techniques and every modern cipher is designed to resist them. Thus, it is shown by the designers that only a few rounds of ASCON and DRYGASCON are vulnerable to these techniques. However, it was shown in [8,24] that the combination of these two methods called the differential-linear cryptanalysis [16] can be used to distinguish 5 rounds of ASCON and DRYGASCON. Although this is not surprising and not against the security claims of the designers, it is surprising that these theoretically obtained distinguishers work a lot better in practice. For instance in [10], although the theoretical bias of a 4-round differential-linear distinguisher is computed as 2^{-20}, it was observed that this bias is actually around 2^{-2} in practice when checked experimentally. This difference between the theory and practice allows the attacker to use less data. Bar-On et al. [1] tried to justify this difference by introducing a table called differential-linear connectivity table (DLTC). This new tool tries to remove the independence assumption between the differential characteristic and the linear approximation. Their analysis provided 2^{-5} bias compared to the theoretical value of 2^{-20}. Thus, [1] tried to explain this phenomenon by showing how the used differential and linear distinguishers affect each other but their approach still is not sufficient to explain the gap between the theoretical results and the practical results because 2^{-5} is still very small compared to the experimental bias of 2^{-2}. Therefore, it is assumed that the large 320-bit internal state and lightweight design of the diffusion and confusion layers of ASCON cause this gap.

Most theoretical attacks are not validated in practice due to required storage and computational power. However, experimentally performing the reduced versions of theoretical attacks can verify the correctness. Moreover, these experiments can be used to correct wrong attacks or improve correct attacks. Thus, experimentally verifying shortened versions of theoretically obtained cryptographic attacks is vital for assessing the security of ciphers.

A preliminary version of this paper [8] appeared in the Proceedings of the 8th International Conference on Information Systems Security and Privacy (ICISSP 2022). In that version we performed a study in order to help the NIST's elimination process. We focused on two competitors: DRYGASCON and ASCON to compare their security due to their similar designs. In our previous work [8], we focused on experimentally validating existing theoretical differential-linear distinguishers of DRYGASCON to compare its security against ASCON. There were practical 4-round and 5-round differential-linear distinguishers for ASCON-128 which can also be used for key recovery attacks on the same number of rounds [24]. For DRYGASCON-128, there was a 5-round theoretical differential-linear distinguisher [24] without the experimental results. When we tried to experimentally validate the existing 5-round differential-linear distinguisher of DRYGASCON in our previous work [8], we realized that the initial 3-round probability one truncated differential distinguisher provided by its designer [21] was erroneous. We also observed that this misinterpretation led to other faulty analyses, which were a 2-round probability one truncated differential distinguisher [24] that was used in a 5-round differential-linear distinguisher and an improved 3.5 round probability one truncated differential distinguisher [24]. The provided 3-round truncated differential distinguisher by its designer [21] and the provided code of DRYGASCON have a different approach for handling the rotations; they moved in the opposite directions. We corrected these analyses and provided them in our study [8]. Moreover, we obtained the 5-round differential-linear distinguisher by activating a single S-box in the input and combined it with a linear approximation that activates a single S-box before the last round. Instead of only checking the theoretically obtained 5-round distinguishers, we used our computational power to experimentally check every 5-round differential-linear distinguisher that has a fixed input difference and an output mask. This approach allowed us to obtain a 5-round practical differential-linear distinguisher of DRYGAS-CON with bias $2^{-5.34}$ [8].

Our preliminary work [8] proved that experimentally checking distinguishers allows us to obtain some of the best distinguishers that cannot be obtained theoretically. With this motivation, in this work we extended our distinguisher search by trying every possible input difference to a single S-box in ASCON and DRYGASCON. This way we first found a better 5-round differential-linear distinguisher for DRYGASCON that has bias $2^{-5.20}$ rather than $2^{-5.34}$. On the other hand, the previous best 5-round differential-linear distinguishers for ASCON had biases $2^{-11.91}$, $2^{-14.87}$, $2^{-15.05}$, and $2^{-8.03}$ when the two key bits for the activated S-box are $(1, 1)$, $(1, 0)$, $(0, 1)$, and $(0, 0)$, respectively [24]. Those distinguishers were designed so that input difference is applied to the nonce and the output mask is observed on the first 64 bits of the output so that they can be converted to key recovery attack. Such distinguishers are called Type-II and removing these constraints mean Type-I distinguishers. In order to better analyze the diffusion and confusion layers of this permutation, we considered the scenarios where the input difference is in the key bits. This resulted in distinguishers with higher biases and such distinguishers can be used for related-key attacks. We further relaxed the places of the output masks and obtained the best 5-round differential-linear distinguishers for ASCON that had biases $2^{-5.40}$, $2^{-5.99}$, $2^{-5.99}$, and $2^{-5.40}$ when the two key bits for the activated S-box are $(1, 1)$, $(1, 0)$, $(0, 1)$, and $(0, 0)$, respectively.

Moreover, the best 5-round differential-linear distinguisher for DRYGASCON which is experimentally obtained in [8] cannot be obtained theoretically. This observation suggests that these lightweight designs might have distinguishers that can only be observed with experiments. Although nobody could obtain a 6-round differential-linear distinguishers for these ciphers yet, this huge difference between the theory and practice suggests that there may be 6-round differential-linear distinguishers for these ciphers that can be obtained experimentally.

In this work, we also optimized ASCON for GPUs using the CUDA language to experimentally find the best 5-round differential-linear distinguishers for the permutations of this cipher. Moreover, we run these optimizations using 2^{48} data to check the existence of 6-round differential-linear distinguishers and observed no distinguishers. With more and better GPUs, more data can be processed to check the existence of 6-round distinguishers. In order to verify our experimental results and promote further research, we made our differential-linear distinguisher search tool publicly available[1].

2   Preliminaries

2.1   Ascon

ASCON [12] is a cipher suite that was not only the primary choice in the CAESAR competition's [2] lightweight applications category, but now is the new lightweight cryptography standard of NIST [20]. It offers authenticated encryption with associated data and hashing capabilities.

ASCON is an algorithm based on substitution-permutation networks (SPNs). Since its mode of operation depends on the type of duplex construction, namely the MonkeyDuplex structure [4], a nonce's uniqueness is necessary for its security. Its encryption procedure consists of four steps: initialization, processing of associated data, processing of plaintext, and finalization.

ASCON has two instances named ASCON-128 and ASCON-128a that differ in data block sizes and round numbers. The primary submission of ASCON, namely ASCON-128, has a 320-bit state formed by five 64-bit words. After 64-bit IV, 128-bit secret key, and 128-bit nonce are formed into a 320-bit state, it is permutated. While the permutation is performed $b = 6$ times in the encryption part, it is performed $a = 12$ times in the initialization and finalization parts. This permutation consists of a constant addition, a substitution layer followed by a diffusion layer. After the substitution layer updates the state 64 times in parallel using a special 5×5 S-box, the diffusion layer applies $\Sigma_i(x_i)$ function to each word. This operation can be described as follows:

$$\Sigma_0(x_0) = (x_0 \ggg 28) \oplus (x_0 \ggg 19) \oplus x_0$$
$$\Sigma_1(x_1) = (x_1 \ggg 39) \oplus (x_1 \ggg 61) \oplus x_1$$
$$\Sigma_2(x_2) = (x_2 \ggg 6) \oplus (x_2 \ggg 1) \oplus x_2$$
$$\Sigma_3(x_3) = (x_3 \ggg 17) \oplus (x_3 \ggg 10) \oplus x_3$$
$$\Sigma_4(x_4) = (x_4 \ggg 41) \oplus (x_4 \ggg 7) \oplus x_4$$

ASCON has been analyzed since 2014, and a summary of these analyzes is published on ASCON's official website[2]. Some of these analyzes were differential linear cryptanalysis [1, 11, 24] regarding key recovery attacks, which we focused on in our study.

---

[1] https://github.com/cihangirtezcan/CUDA_ASCON.

[2] https://ascon.iaik.tugraz.at/publications.html.

2.2 DryGASCON

DRYGASCON [21] is a cipher suite that offers authenticated encryption with associated data and hashing capabilities. It was a contender in the NIST lightweight cryptography competition. Even though it was disqualified after the second round, some designs implemented it [14].

DRYGASCON uses a generalized version of ASCON's permutation, namely $GASCON_{C5R11}$. It uses DrySponge [21] as a mode of operation, a new construction based on Duplex Sponge [3]. Its difference from Duplex Sponge is in combining the input with the state and extracting output from the state. Although DRYGASCON-128 is the primary submission, it has one more instance named DRYGASCON-256.

The permutation of DRYGASCON-128 is very similar to ASCON-128; except the round number of DRYGASCON-128 is 11, not 12. The constant addition depends on the current round, not the total number of rounds. Its S-box is represented in little-endian. Moreover, two rotations of DRYGASCON-128 in the diffusion layer are different, namely Σ_1 and Σ_4. They were changed into 38 from 39 in Σ_1 and 40 from 41 in Σ_4.

Nevertheless, the more significant difference is the rotation function. To ensure that a difference in one half of an input word will be propagated to the other half of the matching output word, each 64-bit word of the state rotates once with an odd shift. This property is not part of the ASCON permutation.

DRYGASCON was analyzed in [8,24] regarding differential-linear cryptanalysis. These analyses focused only on the permutation of DRYGASCON; therefore, they did not consider a unique property of DRYGASCON, namely the $Mix128$ function. With this little tweak, [24] provided a theoretical 5-round differential-linear distinguisher for $GASCON_{C5R11}$. Then [8] improved their results by providing a 5-round practical distinguisher.

2.3 Undisturbed Bits

Undisturbed bits [22] can be seen as a probability one truncated differentials for an S-box. If an output bit's difference remains constant for a specific input difference, it is referred to as being undisturbed. One can utilize undisturbed bits to produce longer and, in some situations, beneficial differentials in truncated, improbable, and impossible differential cryptanalysis.

ASCON has two undisturbed bits in the backward direction and 23 undisturbed bits in the forward direction [23]. DRYGASCON is also subject to the same analysis since it shares the same S-box with ASCON, even though the DRYGASCON represents it in little-endian. The undisturbed bits of both ASCON and DRYGASCON can be seen in Table 1.

Undisturbed bits were used to provide probability one truncated differential distinguishers for ASCON-128 [24], and for DRYGASCON-128 [8,21,24] in the recent studies.

Table 1. Undisturbed bits of DRYGASCON and ASCON's 5 × 5 S-box.

Input Difference	Output Difference	Input Difference	Output Difference
00001	?1???	10000	?10??
00010	1???1	10001	10??1
00011	???0?	10011	0???0
00100	??110	10100	0?1??
00101	1????	10101	????1
00110	????1	10110	1????
00111	0??1?	10111	????0
01000	??11?	11000	??1??
01011	???1?	11100	??0??
01100	??00?	11110	?1???
01110	?0???	11111	?0???
01111	?1?0?		

2.4 Truncated Differential Cryptanalysis

Differential cryptanalysis seeks to determine how a fixed input difference influences the output difference [6]. Truncated differential cryptanalysis [15] is one of the various ways to use this technique. This approach only requires a few bits to be fixed in the input and output differentials; the differences do not need to be fully stated. Undisturbed bits can be utilized for this, and it can be created as probability one for some rounds of the cipher, and that may benefit the creation of differential-linear distinguishers.

In recent studies, 3.5-round [23] and a 3-round [21] probability one truncated differential distinguishers were provided for ASCON and DRYGASCON respectively. This distinguisher of DRYGASCON was improved in [24] to a 3.5-round one. However, both of these distinguishers of DRYGASCON were reported wrong [8], and corrected versions of them were provided in [8]. The reason behind this was the misinterpretation of the diffusion direction of the bits because of the discrepancy between the code and the specification of DRYGASCON.

In our recent study [8], we examined all the probability one truncated differential distinguishers of DRYGASCON-128 [21,23], and realized that all of these were reported wrong due to misinterpretation of the diffusion direction of the bits. We provided the corrected version of these 2, 3, 3.5 round distinguishers in our recent study [8].

2.5 Linear Cryptanalysis

Linear Cryptanalysis [17] seeks a relationship between the plaintext, subkey, and ciphertext bits to get a linear expression of the cipher. This can be accomplished by building a linear approximation table (LAT) using the algorithm's S-box. Since exhaustively searching every linear feature would be computationally impractical, heuristic techniques are a better way to accomplish this. The linear trails tool [10] uses a heuristic approach with various search options for locating suitable characteristics for ASCON based on usage areas, namely Type-I and Type-II. There are no limitations on Type-I characteristics; active bits are allowed to be on any bits of the permutation. Hence, rather than being used to attack a sponge construction, Type-I characteristics can be used to offer an idea about the cipher's resistance to linear cryptanalysis. Type-II characteristics, however, require that the active bits be in the outer part of the state and that no masks should be present in any other bits. Therefore, one can use Type-II characteristics to perform key-recovery attacks on sponge constructions.

In our recent study [8], we used a pre-provided linear characteristics [21] to build differential-linear distinguishers for DRYGASCON-128. We also used the linear trails tool [10] to find both Type-I and Type-II linear approximations of DRYGASCON-128 to build better distinguishers.

In this study, we used the linear trails tool [10] to find better linear characteristics of ASCON-128 and DRYGASCON-128 that would be compatible with their probability one truncated differential distinguishers practically, if not theoretically.

3 Differential-Linear Cryptanalysis

Differential-linear cryptanalysis [16] is a technique for obtaining longer differential-linear distinguishers by combining short differential and linear characteristics. The cipher E is divided into two parts in this technique, namely E_0 and E_1. For the E_0 part, a truncated differential $\lambda_I \rightarrow \lambda_o$ with probability $p = 1$ is used. Then a linear approximation $\nabla_I \rightarrow \nabla_o$ for the E_1 part with probability $1/2 + q$, where q is the bias, is used. Then their combination $E = E_0 \circ E_1$ is used to find a distinguisher for the algorithm. Keep in mind that the output bits of truncated differentials should have a zero difference, matching the masked input bits of the linear approximation.

The idea is to select a suitable number of plaintext pairs with an input difference of λ_I for distinguishing cipher E from a random permutation. Each pair is subjected to the permutation, and it is determined whether the matching ciphertexts $c1, c2$ have the same parity as the mask ∇_o. A sufficient amount of data is used to verify this criterion. As a result, the probability of approximately $1/2$ indicates that the cipher behaves randomly. Otherwise, the cipher might be weak against this technique. The magnitude of this deviation provides insight into how weak the cipher is.

According to [5], this technique still works when the masked bits of the input of linear approximation match with any fixed difference at the output of the differential. In this version, the bias is approximately $2pq^2$, and the data complexity increases to $O(p^{-2}q^{-4})$ chosen plaintexts, where p is less than 1. These computations are based on the piling-up lemma of Matsui [17]. If the probability is $p = 1$, these computations can be shown as $2q^2$ for the bias and $O(q^{-4})$ chosen plaintexts.

In our differential-linear distinguishers we used undisturbed bits to theoretically show that the differentials have fixed differences at the masked input bits of the linear approximation. Furthermore, we relaxed this rule in our experiments in this work because since our experiments provided better probabilities than the theoretically calculated ones, relaxing this condition might allow us to discover better distinguishers in practice which could not be theoretically obtained simply by using undisturbed bits. This way we obtained the best 5-round distinguishers for ASCON.

3.1 Differential-Linear Distinguishers for Ascon

Differential-linear cryptanalysis was applied to 4 and 5 rounds of ASCON-128 to be able to find a suitable distinguisher that might turn into a key-recovery attack [24]. They gave differences to the words x_3 and x_4, namely the nonce, and examined the differences only for x_0 in the output since the plaintext is XORed with it to generate the ciphertext. With this approach, they presented a 4-round differential-linear characteristic with a 2-round Type-II linear approximation with bias 2^{-8} from [10] and a 2-round probability one truncated differential using the undisturbed bits of ASCON [23]. The result of that study [24] showed that the theoretical bias was $2pq^2 = 2 \cdot 1 \cdot 2^{-8} = 2^{-15}$, but the experimentally obtained biases were $2^{-1.68}$, $2^{-2.41}$, $2^{-1.68}$, and $2^{-2.41}$ while key bits are $(1, 1)$, $(1, 0)$, $(0, 1)$, and $(0, 0)$ in the activated S-box, respectively. Slow diffusion and the presence of several linear characteristics were used to explain this discrepancy between theoretical and real biases.

The same input difference is used in [24] to obtain the best known 5-round differential-linear distinguishers for ASCON which had biases of $2^{-11.91}$, $2^{-14.87}$, $2^{-15.05}$, and $2^{-8.03}$ when the two key bits for the activated S-box are $(1, 1)$, $(1, 0)$, $(0, 1)$, and $(0, 0)$, respectively. Thus, this distinguisher has an average bias of $2^{-12.47}$. In this work, we improved these results.

When constructing a differential-linear distinguisher for ASCON, providing an input difference to only a single S-box results in many zero bit differences at the output of the differential. This approach with the use of undisturbed bits allows us to easily combine the differential with a suitable linear approximation which is chosen so that it has small number of input masked bits. Although we obtained 5-round differential-linear distinguisher theoretically this way, in our experiments we performed the same experiment 64 times by providing the input difference to a different S-box in each experiment. In most of these experiments, the differential actually is not suitable with the linear approximation since we cannot guarantee fixed output bit difference that correspond to masked input bits of the linear approximation. However, we obtained the best probabilities from those experiments. Thus, we observed that better distinguishers which cannot be obtained by known theoretical methods can be obtained experimentally.

Although the IV for ASCON is fixed and specified in [12], many cryptographic libraries allow users to select IVs. Thus, in our first round of experiments on ASCON, we chose the input difference as 10011, instead of 00011, which introduces a difference to both IV and the nonce. This input difference has two undisturbed bits, as shown in Table 1. Our experiments showed that the best biases for this input difference are

$2^{-14.45}$, $2^{-12.25}$, $2^{-12.25}$, and $2^{-14.45}$. Thus, this approach makes it easier to capture secret key bits when they are in the form $(0,1)$ or $(1,0)$. When these biases are combined with the 5-round differential-linear distinguishers of [24], average bias can be reduced to $2^{-11.1}$ from $2^{-12.47}$.

We chose the input difference as 01100 in our second round of experiments. This input difference also has two undisturbed bits, as shown in Table 1, and the differences are introduced as secret key bits. Thus, the distinguishers obtained via this input difference can be used in related-key attacks. Our experiments showed that the best biases for this input difference are $2^{-8.52}$, $2^{-7.94}$, $2^{-7.94}$, and $2^{-8.52}$. Thus, such a related-key attack on the 5-round ASCON has at least 2^4 times better bias compared to the 5-round differential-linear attack of [24].

In both of these experiments we used the same linear approximation of [24] which has output mask only in x_0. This allows these distinguishers to turn into attacks because in ASCON ciphertext block is obtained by the XOR of plaintext block with x_0 and therefore the attacker can observe this value. In our final experiments we allowed masked output bits in other x_i to find the best 5-round differential distinguishers for the ASCON permutation. In order to have better transition from differential to linear approximation, we used a linear approximation with small number of input masked bits which is shown in Table 2. This approach provided 5-round differential-linear distinguishers with the best bias of $2^{-5.40}$ when the input difference is 10011 and the secret key is in the form $(0,0)$ or $(1,1)$ and the best bias of $2^{-4.32}$ when the input difference is 01100 and the secret key is in the form $(0,1)$ or $(1,0)$.

Table 2. 2-round Type-I linear characteristic for ASCON-128 permutation with bias 2^{-4} where dots represent unmasked bits.

Round	State
0	....1.C.... ....1.C.... ....
1	....4.... ....
2	DB492DBB69264892 E221EEA5A47CCBA6 .... CC63CDC4B8FEC297

Having 5-round distinguishers with such high biases suggests that the diffusion and the confusion layers of ASCON permutation are not sufficient for 5 rounds. Such high biases also suggests that there might be 6-round differential-linear distinguishers. We experimentally checked the existence of such a distinguisher using 2^{48} data but the observed biases were no different than the biases that can be observed when a random permutation is used. If such a distinguisher exists for 6 rounds, our optimized CUDA codes can detect it when more data is used which requires more time or better or more GPUs.

3.2 Differential-Linear Distinguishers for DryGASCON

A 5-round theoretical differential-linear distinguisher for DRYGASCON was presented in [24]. Since the designer of DRYGASCON stated that the Mix128 function, a unique property of DRYGASCON does not really have any effect on the cipher's security

[21], they [24] worked on the constrained version of the DRYGASCON, namely $GASCON_{C5R11}$. They used a 2-round probability one truncated differential distinguisher together with a 3-round linear approximation with 2^{-15} bias that was provided by the designer [21]. The linear approximation they used was Type-I instead of Type-II, unlike the analysis of ASCON-128. The main idea behind this usage was to give a general opinion about its security against differential-linear cryptanalysis since the attack process would differ due to the additional functions of DRYGASCON. With this in mind, they provided the best distinguisher with an initial difference in x_1 and x_2, instead of x_3 and x_4. The theoretical bias of this operation is said to be $2pq^2 = 2 \cdot 1 \cdot (2^{-15})^2 = 2^{-29}$ with $2^{61.28}$ samples [24], according to Algorithm 1 of [7]. We recently improved this study by experimentally validating this distinguisher [8]. We corrected some erroneous distinguishers from [21,24] and showed that a $2^{-5.35}$ total bias is obtainable with 2^{17} samples for distinguishing 5-round of DRYGASCON, which was significantly better than the theoretical bias 2^{-29} and $2^{61.28}$ data complexity. This experiment was based on using random plaintext pairs and permuted each pair with the specific input differences that might be compatible with the provided linear approximation. Unlike the analysis of ASCON [24], we did not take into account the usage of random nonces and keys because their positions were different in the initial state of DRYGASCON.

Although we worked with specific input differences that we believed would be compatible with linear approximation, they were incompatible. In other words, by using undisturbed bits we could not guarantee fixed output differences on bits that are masked in the input of the linear approximation. But surprisingly, they worked so much better in practice [8]. This situation motivated us to use a more significant initial difference state to find a better distinguisher. Therefore we took all possible 31 S-box values as input differences and rotated them 64 times because DRYGASCON is rotation invariant. Besides, since we used a Type-I linear approach, we were not limited to having masks in certain places. We used 2^{20} random plaintext pairs and permuted each pair with these input differences. Then checked if the corresponding ciphertexts $c1, c2$ had the same parity as the first round of the various 3-round linear approximations that we found using linear trails tool [10]. We calculated their deviation from $1/2$ for each of them to have the best possible bias. Then we observed a 5-round differential-linear distinguisher with bias $2^{-5.2}$, which is better than our previous results $2^{-5.35}$ [8].

In this experiment, we used a 3-round linear approximation with a bias of 2^{-17} and a 2-round probability one truncated differential distinguisher. But note that since this is a practical distinguisher, the masked input bits of the linear approximation do not match the zero difference in the output bits of the truncated differential distinguisher, as can be seen in Table 3. Moreover, our recent linear approximation [8] interestingly had a higher bias than this one; it was 2^{-15}. Still, the approximation with a 2^{-17} bias gave us a better result. This result confirmed our opinion that there are good practical distinguishers we cannot verify in theory but can only be observed with experiments.

Table 3. 5-round practical distinguisher of DRYGASCON with bias $2^{-5.2}$.

Round	2- Round Truncated Differential Distinguisher of $GASCON_{C5R11}$
I	000001000000000000000000000000000000000000000000000000000000000000
	000000000000000000000000000000000000000000000000000000000000000000
	000000000000000000000000000000000000000000000000000000000000000000
	000001000000000000000000000000000000000000000000000000000000000000
	000001000000000000000000000000000000000000000000000000000000000000
S1	000000000000000000000000000000000000000000000000000000000000000000
	00000?000000000000000000000000001000000000000000000000000000000000
	00000?000000000000000000000000000000000000000000000000000000000000
	00000?000000000000000000000000000000000000000000000000000000000000
	000000000000000000000000000000000000000000000000000000000000000000
P1	000000000000000000000000000000000000000000000000000000000000000000
	00000?0000000000000000?0000000000?00000000000000000000000000000000
	00000?00?000000000000000000000000?000000000000000000000000000000000
	00000?0000?0000000000000000000000000?00000000000000000000000000000
	000000000000000000000000000000000000000000000000000000000000000000
S2	00000?00?0?0000000000000?0000000000?0?0000000?000000000000000000000
	00000?00?0?0000000000000?0000000000?0?0000000?000000000000000000000
	00000?00?0?0000000000000?0000000000?0?0000000?000000000000000000000
	00000?00?0?0000000000000?0000000000?0?0000000?000000000000000000000
	00000?0000?000000000000?0000000000?000000000?000000000000000000000
P2	00000??0?0?00?00?0?000?00???00000000?0?0?0000000??00?0?0000000?0000
	00?0??00?0??00000000000?00?0?00?00?0??0?0000?00000000?0?0000000
	0000???0?0?0?0??000000000?00?0000000?0??0?0?00?00?0000000?0000000
	00000?00?0?0?0??,??000000?0?0000?00?00?0?00?0?00?00?0?0000000000000
	00000?0?00?0?0000?000000??0000?00?0?0000?0000?000000000?000?0000

Round	3-Round Linear Approximation of $GASCON_{C5R11}$ with bias 2^{-17}
P2	010000000000100000000000000000001110000000010010000000000000001001
	000000000000000000000000000000000000000000000000000000001000010
	000000000000000000000000000000000000000000000000000000001000010
	000000000000000000000000000000000000000000000000000000000000000000
	010000000000100000000000000000001110000000010010000000000001000
P3	000000000000000000000000000000000000000000000000000000000000000000
	00000000000000000000000000000010000000000000000000000000000001001
	00000000000000000000000000000010000000000000000000000000000001001
	000000000000000000000000000000000000000000000000000000000000000000
	000000000000000000000000000000000000000000000000000000000000000000
P4	000000000000000000000000000000000000000000000000000000000000000000
	000000000000000000000000000000000000000000000000000000000000000000
	000000000000000000000000000000000000000000000000000000000000000001
	000000000000000000000000000000000000000000000000000000000000000000
	000000000000000000000000000000000000000000000000000000000000000000
P5	100101001101100100110111101100100100001001101100100110101100 1001
	111000110111110001001111000110110110110100011010101001111100110
	000000000000000000000000000000000000000000000000000000000000000000
	000000000000000000000000000000000000000000000000000000000000000000
	111100001010000011000001000000010011111000101011111100101010001

4   Conclusions

In recent years, there has been a surge in the number of devices with limited resources, necessitating more lightweight algorithms for cryptographic operations. Even though AES can be optimized for resource-constrained devices, there have been instances where this is impractical. This has led to some platforms using their own poorly analyzed proprietary algorithms. That is why NIST organized a competition to standardize a lightweight algorithm. The selection process took approximately three years, and we performed analyses to help NIST choose the winner in the elimination process [8]. In this work, we studied two similar cipher suites: DRYGASCON and ASCON due to their similar designs, and ASCON was selected as the winner of this competition. The results we obtained from this study are as follows:

– We improved our recent result that has a $2^{-5.34}$ bias [8] by finding a 5-round differential-linear distinguisher with a bias of $2^{-5.2}$ for DRYGASCON-128,
– We provided the best 5-round differential-linear distinguishers for ASCON.
– We provided 5-round related-key differential-linear attacks for ASCON.
– We provided the optimized CUDA codes we used in our study for further analysis and verification.

Our analysis also showed that some lightweight designs might have distinguishers that can only be observed with experiments.

References

1. Bar-On, A., Dunkelman, O., Keller, N., Weizman, A.: DLCT: a new tool for differential-linear cryptanalysis. In: Ishai, Y., Rijmen, V. (eds.) EUROCRYPT 2019. LNCS, vol. 11476, pp. 313–342. Springer, Cham (2019). https://doi.org/10.1007/978-3-030-17653-2_11
2. Bernstein, D.: Caesar: competition for authenticated encryption: Security, applicability, and robustness. https://competitions.cr.yp.to/caesar.html (2013). Accessed 10 May 2021
3. Bertoni, G., Daemen, J., Peeters, M., Van Assche, G.: Duplexing the sponge: single-pass authenticated encryption and other applications. In: Miri, A., Vaudenay, S. (eds.) SAC 2011. LNCS, vol. 7118, pp. 320–337. Springer, Heidelberg (2012). https://doi.org/10.1007/978-3-642-28496-0_19
4. Bertoni, G., Daemen, J., Peeters, M., Van Assche, G.: Permutation-based encryption, authentication and authenticated encryption. Directions in Authenticated Ciphers, pp. 159–170 (2012)
5. Biham, E., Dunkelman, O., Keller, N.: Enhancing differential-linear cryptanalysis. In: Zheng, Y. (ed.) ASIACRYPT 2002. LNCS, vol. 2501, pp. 254–266. Springer, Heidelberg (2002). https://doi.org/10.1007/3-540-36178-2_16
6. Biham, E., Shamir, A.: Differential cryptanalysis of des-like cryptosystems. J. Cryptol. **4**(1), 3–72 (1991)
7. Blondeau, C., Gérard, B., Tillich, J.P.: Accurate estimates of the data complexity and success probability for various cryptanalyses. Designs Codes Crypt. **59**(1), 3–34 (2011)
8. Civek, A.B., Tezcan, C.: Differential-linear attacks on permutation ciphers revisited: experiments on Ascon and DryGASCON. In: Proceedings of the 8th International Conference on Information Systems Security and Privacy, ICISSP 2022, Online Streaming, February 9–11, 2022, pp. 202–209. SCITEPRESS (2022). https://doi.org/10.5220/0010982600003120

9. Daemen, J., Rijmen, V.: The Design of Rijndael: AES - The Advanced Encryption Standard Information Security and Cryptography. Springer, Berlin, Heidelberg (2002). https://doi.org/10.1007/978-3-662-04722-4

10. Dobraunig, C., Eichlseder, M., Mendel, F.: Heuristic tool for linear cryptanalysis with applications to Caesar candidates. In: International Conference on the Theory and Application of Cryptology and Information Security, pp. 490–509. Springer (2015)

11. Dobraunig, C., Eichlseder, M., Mendel, F., Schläffer, M.: Cryptanalysis of ASCON. In: Nyberg, K. (ed.) CT-RSA 2015. LNCS, vol. 9048, pp. 371–387. Springer, Cham (2015). https://doi.org/10.1007/978-3-319-16715-2_20

12. Dobraunig, C., Eichlseder, M., Mendel, F., Schläffer, M.: Ascon v1. 2. Submission to the CAESAR Competition (2016)

13. Eisenbarth, T., Kasper, T., Moradi, A., Paar, C., Salmasizadeh, M., Shalmani, M.T.M.: On the Power of power analysis in the real world: a complete break of the KEELOQ code hopping scheme. In: Wagner, D. (ed.) CRYPTO 2008. LNCS, vol. 5157, pp. 203–220. Springer, Heidelberg (2008). https://doi.org/10.1007/978-3-540-85174-5_12

14. Herndon, R., El-Issa, R., Heer, D., Xiong, J., Hwu, W.-M., El-Hadedy, M.: RECO-DryGASCON: re-configurable lightweight DryGASCON engine. In: Arai, K., Kapoor, S., Bhatia, R. (eds.) FTC 2020. AISC, vol. 1290, pp. 703–721. Springer, Cham (2021). https://doi.org/10.1007/978-3-030-63092-8_47

15. Knudsen, L.R.: Truncated and higher order differentials. In: Preneel, B. (ed.) FSE 1994. LNCS, vol. 1008, pp. 196–211. Springer, Heidelberg (1995). https://doi.org/10.1007/3-540-60590-8_16

16. Langford, S.K., Hellman, M.E.: Differential-linear cryptanalysis. In: Desmedt, Y.G. (ed.) CRYPTO 1994. LNCS, vol. 839, pp. 17–25. Springer, Heidelberg (1994). https://doi.org/10.1007/3-540-48658-5_3

17. Matsui, M.: Linear cryptanalysis method for DES cipher. In: Helleseth, T. (ed.) EURO-CRYPT 1993. LNCS, vol. 765, pp. 386–397. Springer, Heidelberg (1994). https://doi.org/10.1007/3-540-48285-7_33

18. McKay, K., Bassham, L., Sönmez Turan, M., Mouha, N.: Report on lightweight cryptography. Tech. rep, National Institute of Standards and Technology (2016)

19. Meijer, C., Verdult, R.: Ciphertext-only cryptanalysis on hardened mifare classic cards. In: Ray, I., Li, N., Kruegel, C. (eds.) Proceedings of the 22nd ACM SIGSAC Conference on Computer and Communications Security, Denver, CO, USA, October 12–6, 2015, pp. 18–30. ACM (2015). https://doi.org/10.1145/2810103.2813641, http://doi.acm.org/10.1145/2810103.2813641

20. NIST: Lightweight cryptography standardization process: nist selects ascon. https://csrc.nist.gov/News/2023/lightweight-cryptography-nist-selects-ascon (2023). Accessed 17 Apr 2023

21. Riou, S.: Drygascon: a submission to the NIST lightweight cryptography standardization process (2019)

22. Tezcan, C.: Improbable differential attacks on present using undisturbed bits. J. Comput. Appl. Math. **259**, 503–511 (2014)

23. Tezcan, C.: Truncated, impossible, and improbable differential analysis of ascon. In: International Conference on Information Systems Security and Privacy, vol. 2, pp. 325–332. SCITEPRESS (2016)

24. Tezcan, C.: Analysis of ascon, drygascon, and shamash permutations. Int. J. Inf. Secur. Sci. **9**(3), 172–187 (2020)

A Game Theoretic Approach to the Design of Mitigation Strategies for Generic Ransomware

Rudra Prasad Baksi[1(✉)] and Shambhu Upadhyaya[2]

[1] Illinois State University, Normal, IL 61761, USA
rpbaksi@ilstu.edu
[2] University at Buffalo, SUNY, Buffalo, NY 14260, USA
shambhu@buffalo.edu

Abstract. Recently, ransomware attacks have become widespread and are causing unprecedented damage to cyber-physical systems. Although there are various types of ransomware, this paper focuses on a generic version and analyzes it using game theory. When attacked, victims are often faced with the dilemma of deciding whether or not to pay a ransom. To assist victims in making this decision, we develop a game-theoretic model that examines the attack environment and determines the conditions under which the defender has an advantage in neutralizing the attack. We introduce two new parameters to the game model to aid in decision-making when confronted with a ransomware attack. Additionally, we present game models that depict both rational and irrational attacker behavior. We perform a sensitivity analysis on the game model in cases where the attacker behaves rationally, and demonstrate the impact of the parameters on the decision-making process and equilibrium strategies. Ultimately, we explore how the model's outcomes can assist defenders in designing an effective defense system to prevent and mitigate future attacks of a similar nature. This also, prepares the ground for analysis of more advanced form of malware.

Keywords: Cryptography · Computer security · Cybersecurity · Game theory · Ransomware

1 Introduction

Ransomware is a type of malicious software that encrypts important data on a system and demands payment in exchange for access to the data. There are three main types of ransomware: *locker*, *crypto*, and *hybrid* [34]. Locker ransomware blocks the entire system, preventing the user from accessing any of it. Crypto ransomware, on the other hand, only encrypts specific critical data found on the system. Hybrid ransomware combines the capabilities of both locker and crypto ransomware. More recent versions of ransomware have additional features such as campaign abort or a contingency plan in case of discovery prior to the attack launch, making them advanced persistent threats (APT) [7]. However, this paper focuses only on non-APT ransomware to obtain basic results that can be extended to cover more advanced malware and APT-type ransomware in the future.

P. Mori et al. (Eds.): ICISSP 2021/ICISSP 2022, CCIS 1851, pp. 104–124, 2023.
https://doi.org/10.1007/978-3-031-37807-2_6

Ransomware attacks have had a significant impact on both industry and government organizations, causing widespread disruption. These attacks are a major inconvenience that not only disrupt the daily operations of these organizations but also make it challenging for people to carry out their normal activities. These attacks may cause healthcare facilities, schools, public transport organizations, police stations, gas stations, IoT infrastructure of many organizations, and various other institutions to suspend their daily services [23]. In April 2017, the Erie County Medical Center (ECMC) experienced a ransomware attack from a malware known as SamSam. Despite charging a ransom of $30,000 in cryptocurrency, ECMC decided not to comply with the demand and instead ended up spending approximately $10 million on system restoration. However, due to their cyber insurance, ECMC was able to mitigate the financial impact of the attack [13, 16]. In March 2018, the city of Atlanta was also targeted by the SamSam ransomware attack. The city officials made the decision not to pay the ransom demand of $51,000 in cryptocurrency. As a result, the city had to spend an estimated amount ranging from $2.6 million to $17 million to restore its systems. The attack resulted in the loss of years of police data, which was a significant blow to the city's law enforcement capabilities [14, 29]. In May 2021, the Colonial Pipeline, who maintains one of the largest piplines for oil and gas distribution, was targeted by a ransomware attack carried out by a malware known as DarkSide. The attack disrupted the company's operations, and in order to resume operations, Colonial Pipeline paid a ransom of $4.4 million in Bitcoin (75 Bitcoins) to the attackers. This incident sparked a lot of discussions about the growing threat of ransomware attacks and the need for better cybersecurity measures [9]. The attack of DarkSide ransomware on Colonial Pipeline led to fuel shortages in several locations, including cities and airports, and resulted in business losses, public life disruptions, and increased fuel prices. Subsequently, in October 2022, Los Angeles Unified School District (LAUSD) was also targeted by a ransomware attack. It was the 50th attack in 2022 on the U.S. Education system [26]. The healthcare system in India experienced nearly 2 million cyber attacks in the year 2022, originating from over 41,000 unique IP addresses that were linked to various countries in Asia [1]. In November 2022, a ransomware attack hit the All India Institute of Medical Sciences (AIIMS), causing significant disruptions to the medical services provided by the institution [29].

The aforementioned cases are just a few examples of ransomware attacks that countries have recently experienced. However, many attacks remain unreported for various reasons. Nevertheless, the danger posed by ransomware attacks is genuine and the damages inflicted by them are significant. The affected agencies and institutions seek to make prompt and strategic decisions in order to restore services and bring public life back to normalcy. In this context, our paper focuses on decision-making in such situations. The research presented in this paper aims to assist victims in making informed decisions when faced with a ransomware attack.

In our paper, we utilize game theory to analyze a particular type of ransomware, which we refer to as generic ransomware throughout the text. To accomplish this, we construct a sequential game consisting of two players: the attacker and the victim/defender. Through our analysis, we identify optimal strategies for both players and establish equilibrium solutions for various conditions. Additionally, we perform a sensitivity analysis to assess the impact of changes to the decision parameters on the choices made by both players. The primary contribution of our research is the introduction of a parameter for quantifying the value of resources that are under attack, as well as the implementation of a new parameter for enhancing our understanding of the attacker's reputation. As a result, we make both the value of besieged resources and the reputation of the attacker quantifiable metrics that are factored into the decision-making process.

In this paper, we present a game theory model for generic ransomware, wherein the players are choosing their best strategies leading to the equilibrium condition when the players are rational. We also present a ransomware game theory model wherein the attacker behaves irrationally. The paper is organized as follows. In Sect. 2, we discuss some background information and related work on ransomware. In Sect. 3, we present our game theory based analysis of the generic ransomware by starting with a basic game model developed in [8]. We then analyze the results in Sect. 4 and investigate the sensitivity of the values of the parameters while making an informed decision and put forward a prescriptive solution of preparedness and mitigation of the ransomware attack. In this section, we also put forward a game showcasing the irrational behavior of the attacking ransomware. Following this, in Sect. 5, we present a special case of a sophisticated ransomware. Finally, we conclude the paper in Sect. 6 and explore the possibilities of future research in tackling more sophisticated ransomware attacks.

2   Background and Literature Review

The Cyber Kill Chain framework developed by Lockheed Martin describes a seven-stage life cycle of an Advanced Persistent Threat (APT) attack. APT groups create malware that can carry out attacks through multiple stages, and the Cyber Kill Chain provides a framework for understanding these stages [18]. The process of an APT attack is typically conducted through a seven-stage life cycle called the "Cyber Kill Chain" framework, which was developed by Lockheed Martin. The first stage is *reconnaissance phase*, where the attacker gathers information about the target system and scans for vulnerabilities. Next, in the *weaponization phase*, the attacker creates a remote access malware that can enter the system and be controlled remotely. The malware is then delivered to the target system in the delivery phase, followed by the exploitation phase where the vulnerabilities in the system are exploited. The malware escalates its privileges in the *installation phase* and installs backdoors to communicate with the command and control (C&C) centers to receive further instructions. In the *command and control phase*, the attacker uses the remote access malware to affect the target system from the C&C centers. Finally, in the *actions on objective phase*, the attacker carries out the final assault on the target system. LogRhythm defines APTs through a five-stage life cycle [22]. They are also described by Lancaster University through a three stage life cycle [25].

Deception techniques, including honeypots and honeypot farms, have been used by researchers to create defense techniques to thwart attacks. A honeypot is a decoy system or network that is set up to attract and trap attackers. The honeypot is designed to look like a legitimate system or network, but it is actually isolated and monitored by security personnel. A honeypot farm is a group of honeypots that work together to detect and trap attackers. The use of deception techniques can help to distract attackers, slow them down, and gather intelligence about their methods and techniques. This information can then be used to develop more effective defense strategies [24]. They have used proposed adaptive honeypot systems using game theory, wherein the malware would be enticed and eventually leading to the detection of the rootkit malware. Baksi and Upadhyaya [6] presents a hardware-based deception architecture to silently detect and surreptitiously report the same.

Zakaria et al. [34] identified four main areas of research in the field of ransomware: detection, recovery, defense, and prevention. They highlighted the importance of identifying indicators of compromise (IoC), analyzing traffic patterns, and checking malware signatures to detect and prevent ransomware attacks. Additionally, they emphasized the need for effective recovery strategies to minimize the damage caused by such attacks and to prevent future attacks. In our paper, we investigate the strategies of the attacker as well as the defender, and examine "recovery from attack" and "prevention of future attacks" mentioned in [34]. Baksi and Upadhyaya [4] employed a detection method based on Hidden Markov Models (HMM) to detect ransomware attacks. Although originally designed for detecting APT malware, their HMM-based intrusion detection system (IDS) can also be used effectively for detecting generic malware. The defender still remain perplexed about the question regarding the next *plan-of-action*. Baksi and Upadhyaya [6], Cekar et al. [11], and Baksi and Upadhyaya [4] conducted research to address APT-type malware threats, and their proposed defense strategies involve the use of deception. The focus of our paper is on a generic ransomware attack where the defender is put in a vulnerable position, and we propose strategies to assist the defender in making an informed decision. The strategies are designed to be effective in scenarios where deception is not a factor.

The application of game theory has expanded the scope of malware analysis by enabling the examination of the strategies employed by malware and their targets, as well as the investigation of the attack environment. Khouzani et al. [19] proposed a dynamic game-theoretic model based on zero-sum games to address malware attacks. Their approach involves analyzing the structural properties of saddle-point strategies, which are threshold-based policies, to develop a robust defense system against malware attacks. They conducted their analysis on the network defense landscape of mobile wireless networks, focusing on the defender's reception and patching rates and the attacker's annihilation rate of infected nodes. The authors demonstrated that the threshold-based policies provide a robust and effective solution to combat malware attacks using the dynamic game formulation. Spyridopoulos et al. [33] utilized a game-theoretic approach to analyze the cost-benefit of malware proliferation, and used epidemic spread models such as SIR and SIS models. They specifically applied their model to the Code-Red worm and aimed to develop a cost-benefit game-theoretic model that considers malware proliferation strategies like patching and removal of infected nodes in a network. The basis of their model was the "FLIPIT" game. Cekar et al. [11] employed the concept of deception to combat denial of service (DoS) attacks. They utilized a game-theoretic model based on the signaling game with perfect Bayesian equilibrium (PBE) to analyze the effects of deception in countering such attacks. Our paper employs game theory to examine a generic ransomware attack, and we propose two new parameters that can assist the defender in making informed decisions when confronted with such an attack.

Cartwright et al. [10] proposed a game-theoretic model to examine ransomware attacks of a general nature. They used the kidnapping game as the basis for the model [15,27,28]. Cartwright et al. created a game-theoretic model where the malware was represented as a kidnapper and the victim's database was a hostage. Their aim was to assist the defender in deciding whether or not to pay the ransom in a ransomware attack. However, their model was only applicable to attacks where the attacker was governed by the same law as the defender, and they assumed that the attacker could be apprehended to retrieve the ransom payment and the encrypted data. In contrast, our research considers the possibility of attackers being located anywhere in the world during the attack, making it more challenging to apprehend them. We address this issue by using a sequential game to assist the defender in making an informed decision. This approach makes our analysis more generic and applicable to a majority of attacks, especially those staged from foreign lands.

3   Generic Ransomware

3.1   The Threat Landscape Involving Generic Ransomware

A malware is a type of software program created by attackers to cause harm to the victim's system. When the primary goal of the malware is to hijack the victim's resources for a ransom, it is classified as ransomware. Depending on the complexity and level of sophistication, ransomware can be categorized as either APT (Advanced Persistent Threat) or generic. APT ransomware is usually created by nation-state actors and is highly sophisticated and mounted through multiple stages, with monetary gain being the primary goal, while also having other hidden objectives [7]. In contrast, generic ransomware is less complex, and the attacker encrypts the resources and demands a ransom in exchange for releasing them. The sole objective of this type of attack is to make resources inaccessible until the ransom is paid. The basic variant may not be as sophisticated as APT, but it can cause significant harm to organizations and can accumulate a considerable amount of money for the attackers. In this paper, we focus on the generic variant to analyze the ransomware attack and obtain new results compared to previous analyses based on *attack graphs*.

The literature proposes parameterized attack graphs as a means to model vulnerabilities exploited by attacks. These graphs comprise of attacker preconditions, system and network vulnerabilities, attacker effects, and the attack's impact on the network [30]. The attacker precondition includes their capabilities and knowledge needed to stage attacks at an atomic level. However, attack graphs are limited by scalability concerns in both model specification and eventual threat analysis [12]. Although automated tools for attack graph generation [31] exist, such traditional approaches are unsuitable for ransomware attacks where the attacker may use social engineering tactics and launch attacks in multiple stages. To address this limitation, game theory can effectively model ransomware attacks and capture the interactions between the attacker and defender. We introduce two parameters specific to ransomware attacks to facilitate the development of our game model, as described in the following section.

3.2   The Game Model for Generic Ransomware

A game is presented in this section that represents a ransomware attack on a vulnerable and unprepared system. The assumption is that the attacker has exploited a vulnerability, leaving the defender with no time to prepare. After the attack, the defender is faced with two options: pay the ransom and hope for the release of the decryption key, or not pay the ransom. The defender can make these choices based on certain conditions, and two conditions are analyzed in this section to assist the defender in making an informed decision on whether to pay the ransom and decrypt the encrypted resources. According to the assumptions, the defender's *willingness* to pay the ransom depends primarily on two factors: the value of the resources held for ransom and the reputation of the attacker.

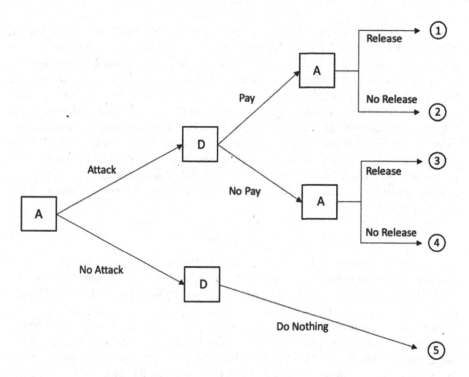

Fig. 1. A Generic Ransomware Attack [8].

Baksi and Upadhyaya presented a similar scenario to the generic ransomware, called the basic ransomware, in their work [8]. They showed a game model in Fig. 1, where the attacker starts by choosing between two strategies, "Attack" or "No Attack". If the attacker chooses to attack, the vulnerable resources are encrypted, and the defender is left with two options, "Pay" or "No Pay". After the defender's move, the attacker has two strategies to choose from, "Release" or "No Release" of the decryption key. If the attacker is rational, they will only release the decryption key if the ransom is paid, otherwise, they won't. However, in some cases, the attacker may choose to act irrationally, but this is not within the scope of this paper. The reputation of the attacker plays an important role in the defender's decision-making process as it can help them make an informed decision when under attack.

The eq. (1) contains a parameter r_{Rec} which represents the proportion of recovered resources after paying the ransom to the total value of the defender's assets. The variable R represents the value of resources at risk, and β represents the ransom amount charged by the attacker. The value of recovered resources can be calculated as $R - \beta$. The total value of the defender's assets is represented by $R_{Total Assets}$. Thus, r_{Rec} indicates how important it is for the defender to recover the resources, given the total value of assets, assuming that the encrypted resources have been released after paying the ransom.

$$r_{Rec} = \frac{R - \beta}{R_{Total Assets}} \tag{1}$$

In eq. (2), the parameter r_{Rep} represents the attacker's reputation as a rational or irrational player in the game. A higher value of r_{Rep} indicates a more rational and trustworthy attacker. For a given incident, the attacker's reputation is determined by assigning a value of 1 if they release the decryption key upon receiving the ransom payment or if they do not release the decryption key when the defender does not pay the ransom. For all other cases, a value of 0 is assigned for the reputation of that incident. The overall reputation of the attacker is calculated by taking the mean of the reputation values of all the reported incidents. In the case of a first-time attack, a value of 0.5 is assigned to r_{Rep} for decision-making purposes. If the attackers act rationally, their r_{Rep} value increases for the next game. However, if they act irrationally, they receive a penalty and their r_{Rep} value decreases, resulting in a lower willingness of the defender to pay the ransom.

$$r_{Rep} = [Mean\ of\ all\ last\ known\ reported\ incidents] \tag{2}$$

The utility functions and strategies of the attacker and defender for the generic ransomware campaign being studied in this paper are described using notations listed in Tables 1 and 2, similar to the basic ransomware campaign portrayed by Baksi and Upadhyaya [8].

The paper examines the strategies of the attacker and defender, taking all relevant parameters into account. The attacker's strategy is represented by variable x_1, which can either be "Attack" or "No Attack". The value of 1 is assigned to "Attack" when the attacker chooses to attack, and 0 otherwise. Similarly, the value of 1 is assigned to "No Attack" when there is no attack, and 0 otherwise. Another variable, x_2, represents the attacker's decision to "Release" or "No Release" the decryption key. The value of 1 is assigned to "Release" when the attacker chooses to release the decryption key, and 0 otherwise. Similarly, the value of 1 is assigned to "No Release" when the attacker chooses not to release the decryption key, and 0 otherwise. On the other hand, the defender's decision is represented by variable y, which can either be "Pay" or "No Pay". The value of 1 is assigned to "Pay" when the defender decides to pay the

Table 1. Attacker Notations [8].

Notation	Description
x_1, x_2	Attacker's first and second strategies, respectively
$x^*, \widehat{x}$	Optimal strategy and best response, respectively
U_A, U_A^*	Expected Utility and Optimal Utility, respectively
Release	Decision to release the encryption keys (value 0 or 1)
(1-Release)	Decision to not release the encryption keys (No Release)

Table 2. Defender Notations [8].

Notation	Description
y	Defender's Strategy
$y^*, \widehat{y}$	Optimal strategy and best response, respectively
U_D, U_D^*	Expected Utility and Optimal Utility, respectively
Pay	Decision to pay the ransom (value 0 or 1)
(1-Pay)	Decision to not pay the ransom (No Pay)

ransom, and 0 otherwise. Similarly, the value of 1 is assigned to "No Pay" when the defender decides against payment of the ransom, and 0 otherwise. The utility functions of the attacker and the defender are defined by setting $x_1 = Attack$, $y = Pay$, and $x_2 = Release$, which are given by equations (3) and (4), respectively. Tables 1 and 2 list the notations used to describe the strategies and utility functions of the attacker and the defender in a generic ransomware campaign, similar to the basic ransomware campaign depicted by Baksi and Upadhyaya [8].

$$
\begin{aligned}
U_D \equiv (x_1) * [&(y) * \{(x_2) * (R - \beta) \\
&+ (1 - x_2) * (-R - \beta)\} \\
&+ (1 - y) * \{(x_2) * (R) + (1 - x_2) * (-R)\}] \\
&+ (1 - x_1) * (0)
\end{aligned}
\tag{3}
$$

$$
\begin{aligned}
U_A \equiv (x_1) * [&(y) * \{(x_2) * (\beta) \\
&+ (1 - x_2) * (\beta)\} + (1 - y) * \{(x_2) * (0) \\
&+ (1 - x_2) * (0)\}] \\
&+ (1 - x_1) * (\lambda)
\end{aligned}
\tag{4}
$$

The above equations show all strategies and all scenarios including the ones which generated a pay-off of 0 for the player. The simplified equations are:

$$
\begin{aligned}
U_D \equiv (x_1) * [&(y) * \{(x_2) * (R - \beta) + (1 - x_2) * (-R - \beta)\} \\
&+ (1 - y) * \{(x_2) * (R) + (1 - x_2) * (-R)\}]
\end{aligned}
\tag{5}
$$

$$U_A \equiv (x_1) * [(y) * \{(x_2) * (\beta) + (1 - x_2) * (\beta)\}]$$
$$+(1 - x_1) * (\lambda) \tag{6}$$

The defender considers both the recovered resources and the attacker's reputation before deciding whether to pay the ransom or not. If the values of r_{Rec} and r_{Rep} are significantly high, the defender should pay the ransom, whereas if they are significantly low, the defender should not pay. Table 3 presents four different scenarios for different values of r_{Rec} and r_{Rep}. The threshold values for r_{Rec} and r_{Rep} are predetermined by the defender, and they are based on the total value of assets the defender owns. If $r_{Rec} \geq t_{Rec}$, it is considered to have a "High (H)" value, otherwise, it is considered to have a "Low (L)" value. Similarly, if $r_{Rep} \geq t_{Rep}$, it is considered to have a "High (H)" value, otherwise, it is considered to have a "Low (L)" value. Having predetermined threshold values helps the defender in attack preparedness and making economic decisions with contingency plans in place.

Table 3. Recovered Resources and Reputation Value for Defender [8].

		Value of Affected Resources (r_{Rec})	
		High (H)	Low (L)
Reputation (r_{Rep})	High (H)	H, H	H, L
	Low (L)	L, H	L, L

After establishing the players' strategies and utility functions, we will now explain the decision-making process and the game's progression, followed by presenting equilibrium solutions based on various conditions. Next, we will conduct a sensitivity analysis to assist the defender in understanding how parameter changes affect the decision-making process. A modification in the value of the parameter r_{Rec} implies a change in the defender's valuation of encrypted resources. A change in r_{Rec} can occur due to changes in R, β, or $R_{TotalAssets}$. This analysis will assist the defender in attack readiness, and the impact of parameter changes on the decision-making process will be evident from the sensitivity analysis.

4 Basic Results for Generic Ransomware

4.1 Conditions for Decision Making

The pay-off for both the defender and the attacker in various scenarios is displayed in Table 4. If the attacker chooses to initiate an attack, the maximum pay-off for them would be the ransom amount they receive, which is denoted as $U_A(x_1 = Attack) = \beta$. This ransomware primarily aims for financial gain through the ransom paid by the victims. If the attacker opts not to attack, their pay-off would be the amount they save by avoiding the cost of the attack, represented as $U_A(x = No; Attack) = \lambda$.

Table 4. Pay-off table for generic ransomware attack game [8].

Outcome	Attacker	Defender
1	β	$R - \beta$
2	β	$-R - \beta$
3	0	R
4	0	$-R$
5	λ	0

For $x_1 = Attack$ the following condition must hold,

$$F_1 \equiv U_A(x = Attack) \geq U_A(x = No\ Attack) \equiv \beta \geq \lambda$$

For $x_1 = No\ Attack$ the following condition must hold,

$$F_2 \equiv U_A(x = Attack) < U_A(x = No\ Attack) \equiv \beta < \lambda$$

From the conditions F_1 and F_2 we get,

$$x_1^* = \begin{cases} \text{``Attack''} & \beta \geq \lambda \\ \text{``No Attack''} & \text{Otherwise} \end{cases} \tag{7}$$

For $x_2 = Release$ or $x_2 = No\ Release$ the following condition should hold so that it is in the best interest of the attacker,

$$x_2^* = \begin{cases} \text{``Release''} & y = \text{``Pay''} \\ \text{``No Release''} & \text{Otherwise} \end{cases} \tag{8}$$

The pay-off table enables the attacker to make informed decisions. The attacker has the advantage of making the first move and when they decide to attack, the defender must choose whether or not to pay the ransom. Once the defender has made their decision, the attacker determines whether or not to release the decryption key, effectively ending the game. In contrast, the defender's decision is not as straightforward. The pay-off table does not account for the defender's resource value, and it does not provide any information about the attacker's rationality or reputation. As a result, the defender must consider other factors. To address this issue, this paper introduces two parameters, namely r_{Rec} and r_{Rep}, to assist the defender in making an informed decision.

The defender establishes the threshold for both parameters, and if a parameter's value surpasses the threshold, it is considered to have a "High (H)" value, while values lower than the threshold are deemed "Low (L)". After determining the values for both parameters, the defender should refer to Table 3 to reach a decision. Therefore, the optimal strategy is

$$y^* = \begin{cases} \text{``Pay''} & r_{Rec} \geq t_{Rec}\ \text{AND}\ r_{Rep} \geq t_{Rep} \\ \text{``No Pay''} & r_{Rec} < t_{Rec}\ \text{OR}\ r_{Rep} < t_{Rep} \end{cases} \tag{9}$$

4.2 Solutions Obtained Through Equilibrium Conditions and Strategies

The game includes conditions, strategies, and pay-offs for each strategy, and Table 5 and Fig. 2 provide the optimal responses for both the attacker and the defender based on these factors. These optimal responses translate to equilibrium solutions for the game given the conditions. Figure 3 illustrates the potential outcomes when the attacker acts irrationally, such as withholding the decryption key even after receiving the ransom payment or releasing the decryption key before receiving payment. However, our analysis in this paper only considers a rational attacker.

Table 5. Best Response of the Attacker and the Defender given the conditions (Equilibrium Strategies) [8].

Conditions		Strategies	
Attacker	Defender	Attacker($\widehat{x_1}, \widehat{x_2}$)	Defender($\widehat{y}$)
$\beta < \lambda$	N/A	No Attack, Nothing	Do Nothing
$\beta \geq \lambda$	$r_{Rep} \geq t_{Rep}$ AND $r_{Rec} \geq t_{Rec}$	Attack, Release	Pay
$\beta \geq \lambda$	$r_{Rep} < t_{Rep}$ OR $r_{Rec} < t_{Rec}$	Attack, No Release	No Pay

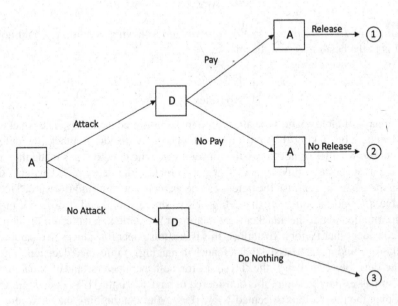

Fig. 2. Game Model for Equilibrium Strategies.

Parameter λ represents the cost of an attack for the attacker. If the attacker chooses not to attack, represented by the strategy "No Attack", the pay-off is λ, which reflects the money saved by avoiding the cost of an attack. A higher value of λ indicates a

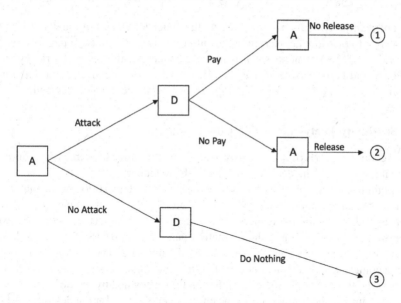

Fig. 3. Game Model when the attacker behaves irrationally.

more difficult system to infiltrate, which would discourage the attacker from initiating an attack. This information is crucial for the defender, as it incentivizes them to employ a robust encryption system to secure the database and implement security best practices to reduce the number of system vulnerabilities.

In the event of an attack, the defender is faced with a decision to either "Pay" or "Not Pay". This is where the threshold values for r_{Rec} and r_{Rep} come into play during the decision-making process. The defender must determine a value for t_{Rec} based on the value of the resources at risk and the total value of all their resources, which helps establish a ransom payment limit that the defender is comfortable with. As r_{Rec} falls below t_{Rec} for various resource values, ransom amounts, and total assets, the willingness to pay the ransom decreases because the value of the recovered resources becomes less important to the defender.

The defender cannot solely rely on the r_{Rec} parameter to make the decision whether to pay the ransom or not. It is equally important to consider the reputation of the malware. If r_{Rec} is below the threshold t_{Rec}, then the defender may choose not to pay the ransom if the resources under attack are not that valuable. However, if r_{Rec} is equal to or greater than t_{Rec}, the defender should check the value of r_{Rep}. If r_{Rep} is below the threshold t_{Rep}, then the reputation of the malware is poor, and the attacker may not release the decryption key even after payment. On the other hand, if r_{Rep} is greater than or equal to t_{Rep}, then the reputation of the malware is good, and paying the ransom may result in the attacker releasing the decryption key. The best course of action for the defender is to pay the ransom when $r_{Rec} \geq t_{Rec}$ and $r_{Rep} \geq t_{Rep}$, and not to pay otherwise.

If the attacker perceives that the reward is greater when choosing $x_1 = Attack$ rather than $x_1 = No\ Attack$, then they will launch the attack. In the case of the ransomware examined in this paper, assuming the attacker behaves rationally, it is in their best interest to provide the decryption key after receiving the ransom payment, and not to provide it if the payment is not made. Consequently, the optimal strategy for the attacker would be to choose $\widehat{x_1}$, $\widehat{x_2} = Attack$, $Release$ upon receiving the ransom payment and $\widehat{x_1}$, $\widehat{x_2} = Attack$, $No\ Release$ if the payment is not received.

4.3   Sensitivity Analysis to Validate the Results

In this section, we perform a sensitivity analysis to determine how the values of ransom and total assets affect the decision making of the defender.

Assuming our organization has a total asset value of \$10,000 and of that, \$1,000 worth of resources come under siege. We set the threshold values for recovered resources and reputation parameters at 0.05 and 0.5, respectively. Additionally, we set the ransom value at \$300 and the reputation parameter at 0.618. To analyze how the decision-making process changes with the total value of assets, we vary $R_{TotalAssets}$ while keeping other parameters constant. When the value of $R_{TotalAssets}$ is \$14,000, r_{Rec} is at the threshold. By increasing the total assets owned by the defender, we visualize the change in the importance of the encrypted resources for the defender. A higher value of r_{Rec} implies that the encrypted resources are more important for the defender. The decision of the defender is shown in Fig. 4b, where a decision to pay is represented by 1 and not to pay is represented by 0. It can be observed that as the importance of encrypted resources decreases, the willingness to pay the ransom also decreases. It is evident from equation (1) and Fig. 4a that r_{Rec} is inversely related to $R_{TotalAssets}$.

Now we vary the ransom value. Let's start by varying the ransom value from \$100 to \$1,000, while keeping the value of R at \$1,000, t_{Rec} 0.05, t_{Rep} 0.5, and r_{Rep} 0.618. We use these parameters to see how the increasing ransom value affects the decision-making process. Figure 5a shows the changes in the r_{Rec} value. When the ransom value is at \$500, r_{Rec} is at the threshold. We observe that increasing the value of the ransom diminishes the effective value of the recovered resources. This leads to a reduction in their importance to the defender, resulting in a decreased willingness to pay the ransom. Figure 5b shows how the decision of the defender changes with the increase in the ransom value. We denote the decision to pay the ransom as 1 and the decision not to pay as 0. As the value of the ransom increases, the defender becomes less willing to pay, due to the decreasing effective value of the recovered resources. We can see from equation (1a) and Fig. 5a that the relationship between r_{Rec} and β is linear with a negative slope.

The sensitivity analysis demonstrates how we can assess the significance of each parameter in the decision-making process. Although we provided a sample scenario with artificial data in this paper, it can be used in real-world situations by inputting actual values. This process of decision-making aids in making an educated decision when confronted with an attack. The sensitivity analysis allows us to comprehend the impact of the attack, and it facilitates the defender's preparedness against the attack.

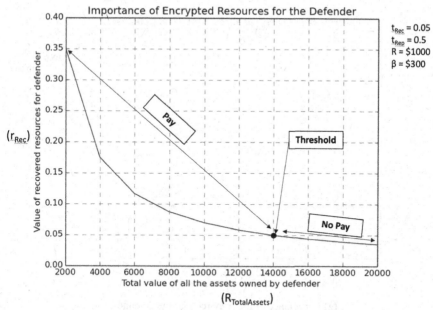

(a) Importance of the resources for the defender

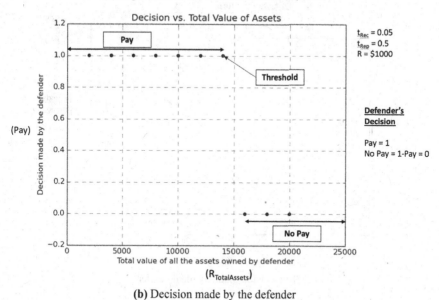

(b) Decision made by the defender

Fig. 4. Sensitivity Analysis by varying $R_{TotalAssets}$ [8].

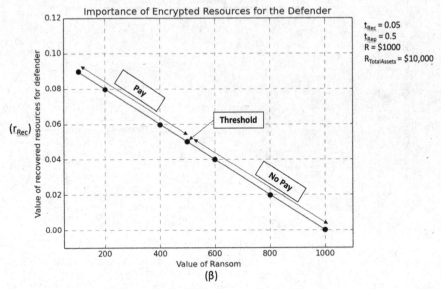

(a) Importance of the resources for the defender

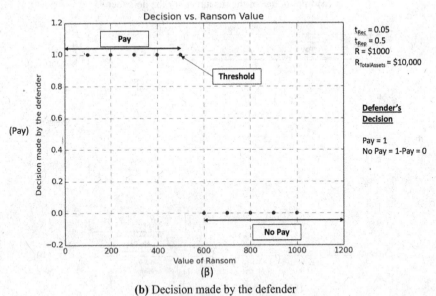

(b) Decision made by the defender

Fig. 5. Sensitivity Analysis by varying Ransom Value [8].

4.4 Prescriptive Solution

In Sect. 4.3, the sensitivity analysis demonstrates how altering the ransom value or the total asset value owned by the defender can impact their decision-making process. The equilibrium strategies for both the attacker and defender are outlined in Table 5, which was obtained using backward induction without any data. While the sensitivity analysis was based on a specific dataset, the game can be applied to any range of data for a generic ransomware attack. However, obtaining data on ransomware attacks can be difficult as institutions and organizations may be hesitant to report details due to concerns about sensitive information being leaked or negative impacts on their reputation. As a result, it may be argued that this is an incomplete information game [17]. However, some values such as λ and r_{Rep}, as discussed in Sect. 4.3, can be estimated through penetration testing, ethical hacking, or researching historical attacks [21] [35]. If no information is available, r_{Rep} can be assumed to be 0.5. Therefore, with the values considered and assumptions made, Table 5 and Algorithm 1 provide a prescriptive solution for a generic ransomware attack. The equilibrium strategies and algorithm offer a means for the defender to prepare in advance and make informed decisions when confronted with a ransomware attack.

Algorithm 1. Choosing Defender's strategy based on the Optimized Strategy of Attacker from Table 5.

$t_{Rec} = \#$ Set by Defender based on system config.
$t_{Rep} = \#$ Set by Defender based on info collected
if $\beta \geq \lambda$ **then**
    if $r_{Rec} \geq t_{Rec}$ AND $r_{Rep} \geq t_{Rep}$ **then**
        return Pay
    else
        return No Pay
    end if
else if $\beta < \lambda$ AND $\widehat{x_1} = No\ Attack$ **then**
    return Do Nothing
end if

The generic ransomware attack may include additional features, such as an early ransom payment deadline that results in doubling the ransom amount after the deadline. In such cases, the defender can update the relevant parameter values, including the ransom value, accordingly. Another potential feature is a bargaining stage between the attacker and defender, which would allow for parameter updates if the ransom value or the value of the targeted resources change. The value of r_{Rep} can be calculated using previous ransomware attacks that are known to the defender or have been publicly reported, as demonstrated in eq. (2). If no historical data is available, a default value of 0.5 can be used for r_{Rep}. However, if any information linking the ongoing attack to a previous attack or attacker is discovered, the defender can update eq. (2) accordingly and adjust the parameter values and tables in the game accordingly.

With the updated game, the defender can consult Table 5 and Algorithm 1 to make an informed decision. By implementing a robust security system, efficient intrusion detection system, powerful encryption system, and following appropriate security protocols, the defender enhances the value of λ. This, in turn, acts as a deterrent against potential attacks on the system.

In the next section, we show how the model presented for generic ransomware analysis can inspire analysis of a special ransomware. The special ransomware discussed in Sect. 5 is of the type APT.

5   A Special Case: APT Type Ransomware

Malware created by the Advanced Persistent Threat (APT) groups do not typically carry out the attacks in a single stage. The "Cyber Kill Chain" framework developed by Lockheed Martin describes an APT through a seven stage life cycle [18]. APT groups are generally nation state actors [2]. They perform highly targeted attacks and do not stop until the goal is achieved [32]. Researchers are always working toward developing a system and a process to create an environment safe from APT type attacks [3]. In this paper, the threat considered is ransomware which are developed by APT groups. WannaCry is an example of a highly sophisticated ransomware created by the Lazurus group of North Korea and its level of sophistication is evident from the existence of a contingency plan of attack upon being discovered [7] [20].

An APT ransomware possesses advanced capabilities and resources, and conducts targeted attacks with an ulterior motive to gain access to encrypted resources. Despite being a ransomware, the attacker may refuse to release the encrypted files even after receiving the ransom, if it believes it would benefit more by keeping the resources for itself. Since the ransomware attack is the primary mode of attack, the highest payoff is obtained by encrypting the target resources. Additionally, the attacker, being an APT

Table 6. Strategies & Notations & Parameters - Defender against APT attack [5].

Strategies & Parameters	Definition
Pay (P)	Pays the ransom
No Pay (NP)	Doesn't pay the ransom (1-P)
Surrender (S)	Surrenders to the contingency attack
No Surrender (NS)	Doesn't surrender to contingency attack (1-S)
g	Damage suffered due to "No Surrender" strategy
g_A	Damage due to "Campaign Abort" strategy
g_C	Damage suffered due to "Campaign Complete" strategy
c	Damage suffered due to "Surrender" strategy
c_A	Damage due to "Campaign Abort" strategy
c_C	Damage suffered due to "Campaign Complete" strategy
R	Value of the resources under risk
d	Cost of implementing deception and back-up mechanism
P_D	Probability of discovery and having deception mechanism

type malware, can perform contingency attacks when it senses that it has been discovered or is at risk of being discovered, due to its abundance of resources.

We make an assumption that the defender may use an intrusion detection system (IDS) that employs deception as a defense strategy, as described in [4]. However, IDSes

Table 7. Strategies & Notations & Parameters - APT Attacker [5].

Strategies & Parameters	Definition
Ransomware (RW)	Ransomware type attack
Contingency Attack (CT)	Mounts a different form of attack
Campaign Abort (CA)	Aborts the ongoing attack
Campaign Complete (CC)	Completes the ongoing attack
Release (R)	Releases the encrypted resources
No Release (NR)	Releases the encrypted resources
β	Ransom charged for the encrypted resources
γ	Advantage parameter for *"Not Releasing"* the key
λ	Cost of *attack*
δ	Gain from "Campaign Abort" strategy
ω	Gain from "Campaign Complete" strategy
P_P	Perception probability regarding deception mechanism

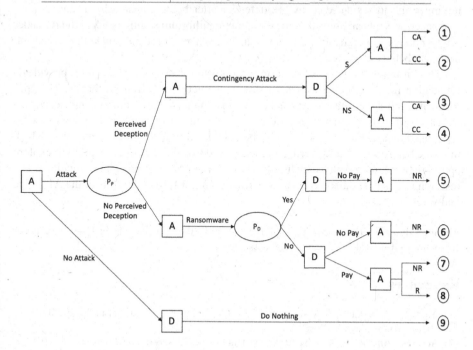

Fig. 6. APT Type Ransomware Game.

are not perfect and a successful deception and discovery mechanism indicates that the malware has been detected and the defender has been covertly alerted of the intrusion. Moreover, if the defender successfully detects and discovers the ransomware, it means that the critical data was backed up through the defender's backup strategy.

The assumptions mentioned earlier will set the foundation for the game played between the attacker and the defender. The defender's strategies and payoff parameters are summarized in Table 6, while the attacker's strategies and payoff parameters are summarized in Table 7. The sequential game depicting an APT type ransomware is shown in Fig. 6. The detailed analysis of the sophisticated ransomware of the APT variant using game theory is more complex and is outside the scope of this paper.

6 Conclusions and Future Work

This paper uses game theory to analyze a generic version of ransomware and its attack landscape. The study considers the actions of both the attacker and the victim, and introduces two parameters to aid the defender in making informed decisions. The first parameter, r_{Rec}, represents the ratio of the value of recovered resources after paying the ransom to the total value of all the assets owned by the defender. This helps the defender quantify the importance of the resources being held hostage. The higher the value of r_{Rec}, the more likely the defender is to pay the ransom. The second parameter, r_{Rep}, quantifies the reputation or trustworthiness of the ransomware. The higher the reputation, the more likely the defender is to pay the ransom. Both parameters aim to minimize the losses suffered by the defender after being attacked by a ransomware. The paper presents an algorithm for obtaining equilibrium solutions when the defender is under attack from ransomware, and includes game models depicting both rational and irrational behaviors on the part of the attacker.

The formal analysis of the generic ransomware presented in this paper provides a foundation for developing mitigation strategies to counter advanced threats. The approach, methodology, and results can be used in conjunction with more complex sequential games to analyze and mitigate more sophisticated ransomware attacks, such as APT-type ransomware. Future research will be conducted to determine the extent to which malware behaves rationally during an attack. Additionally, our future work will explore appropriate threshold values, including any necessary psychological investigations. The research in this paper also serves as a starting point for further analysis of the APT-type malware.

Acknowledgment. This research is supported in part by the National Science Foundation under Grant No. DGE –1754085. Usual disclaimers apply.

References

1. Ahaskar, A.: Indian healthcare sector suffers 1.9 million cyberattacks in 2022. MINT (12 2022). https://shorturl.at/msDET
2. Auty, M.: Anatomy of an advanced persistent threat. Netw. Secur. **2015**(4), 13–16 (2015)
3. Baize, E.: Developing secure products in the age of advanced persistent threats. IEEE Secur. Priv. **10**(3), 88–92 (2012). https://doi.org/10.1109/MSP.2012.65

4. Baksi, R.P., Upadhyaya, S.J.: Decepticon: a theoretical framework to counter advanced persistent threats. Inf. Syst. Front., 1–17 (2020)
5. Baksi, R.P.: Pay or not pay? a game-theoretical analysis of ransomware interactions considering a defender's deception architecture. In: 2022 52nd Annual IEEE/IFIP International Conference on Dependable Systems and Networks-Supplemental Volume (DSN-S), pp. 53–54. IEEE (2022)
6. Baksi, R.P., Upadhyaya, S.J.: Kidemonas: the silent guardian. Secure Knowl. Manage. (SKM '17), Tampa, FL (10 2017)
7. Baksi, R.P., Upadhyaya, S.J.: A comprehensive model for elucidating advanced persistent threats (APT). In: Proceedings of the International Conference on Security and Management (SAM), pp. 245–251. The Steering Committee of The World Congress in Computer Science, Computer Enigineering (2018)
8. Baksi, R.P., Upadhyaya, S.J.: Game theoretic analysis of ransomware: a preliminary study. In: ICISSP, pp. 242–251 (2022)
9. BBC: Colonial pipeline boss confirms $4.4M ransom payment. The British Broadcasting Corporation (05 2021). https://www.bbc.com/news/business-57178503
10. Cartwright, E., Hernandez Castro, J., Cartwright, A.: To pay or not: game theoretic models of ransomware. J. Cybersecur. 5(1), tyz009 (2019)
11. Çeker, H., Zhuang, J., Upadhyaya, S., La, Q.D., Soong, B.-H.: Deception-based game theoretical approach to mitigate dos attacks. In: Zhu, Q., Alpcan, T., Panaousis, E., Tambe, M., Casey, W. (eds.) GameSec 2016. LNCS, vol. 9996, pp. 18–38. Springer, Cham (2016). https://doi.org/10.1007/978-3-319-47413-7_2
12. Chinchani, R., Iyer, A., Ngo, H., Upadhyaya, S.: Towards a theory of insider threat assessment. In: 2005 International Conference on Dependable Systems and Networks (DSN'05), pp. 108–117 (2005). https://doi.org/10.1109/DSN.2005.94
13. Davis, H.L.: How ECMC got hacked by cyber extortionists – and how it's recovering. The Buffalo News (05 2017). https://buffalonews.com/business/local/how-ecmc-got-hacked-by-cyber-extortionists-and-how-its-recovering/article_bfdd8b2e-d3e3-5750-9329-2c20e8634a70.html
14. Deere, S.: Confidential report: Atlanta's cyber attack could cost taxpayers $17 million. The Atlanta Journal Constitution (08 2018). https://www.wired.com/story/atlanta-spent-26m-recover-from-ransomware-scare/
15. Gintis, H.: Game Theory Evolving. Princeton University Press, Princeton (2009)
16. Goud, N.: ECMC spends $10 million to recover from a cyber attack! Cyber Security Insider (2017). https://www.cybersecurity-insiders.com/ecmc-spends-10-million-to-recover-from-a-cyber-attack/
17. Harsanyi, J.C.: Games with incomplete information. In: Evolution and Progress in Democracies, pp. 43–55. Springer (1994). https://doi.org/10.1007/978-94-017-1504-1_2
18. Hutchins, E.M., Cloppert, M.J., Amin, R.M.: Intelligence-driven computer network defense informed by analysis of adversary campaigns and intrusion kill chains. Leading Issues Inf. Warfare Secur. Res. 1(1), 80 (2011)
19. Khouzani, M., Sarkar, S., Altman, E.: A dynamic game solution to malware attack. In: 2011 Proceedings IEEE INFOCOM, pp. 2138–2146. IEEE (2011)
20. Kim, Y.K., Lee, J.J., Go, M.H., Lee, K.: Analysis of the asymmetrical relationships between state actors and apt threat groups. In: 2020 International Conference on Information and Communication Technology Convergence (ICTC), pp. 695–700 (2020). https://doi.org/10.1109/ICTC49870.2020.9289506
21. Krishnan, S., Wei, M.: Scada testbed for vulnerability assessments, penetration testing and incident forensics. In: 2019 7th International Symposium on Digital Forensics and Security (ISDFS), pp. 1–6. IEEE (2019)

22. LogRhythm: the apt lifecycle and its log trail. Tech. Rep. (July 2013)
23. Milosevic, J., Sklavos, N., Koutsikou, K.: Malware in IoT software and hardware. Workshop on Trustworthy Manufacturing and Utilization of Secure Devices (TRUDEVICE'16), Barcelona, Spain (2016)
24. Pauna, A.: Improved self adaptive honeypots capable of detecting rootkit malware. In: 2012 9th International Conference on Communications (COMM), pp. 281–284. IEEE (2012)
25. Rashid, A., et al.: Detecting and preventing data exfiltration (2014)
26. Romine, T., Sanchez, R., Razek, R.: Cybercriminals behind Los Angeles unified school district ransomware attack release hacked data, superintendent says. CNN (10 2022). https://www.cnn.com/2022/10/01/us/los-angeles-unified-school-district-ransomware-attack/index.html
27. Selten, R.: A simple game model of kidnapping. In: Mathematical Economics and Game Theory, pp. 139–155. Springer (1977). https://doi.org/10.1007/978-3-642-45494-3_11
28. Selten, R.: A simple game model of kidnapping. In: Models of strategic rationality, pp. 77–93. Springer (1988). https://doi.org/10.1007/978-94-015-7774-8_4
29. Sen, S.R., Pradhan, B.: Hackers cripple prestigious Indian hospital's it systems. Bloomberg (11 2022). https://www.bloomberg.com/news/articles/2022-11-29/hackers-cripple-prestigious-indian-hospital-s-internet-systems?leadSource=uverify%20wall
30. Sheyner, O., Haines, J., Jha, S., Lippmann, R., Wing, J.: Automated generation and analysis of attack graphs. In: Proceedings 2002 IEEE Symposium on Security and Privacy, pp. 273–284 (2002). https://doi.org/10.1109/SECPRI.2002.1004377
31. Sheyner, O., Wing, J.: Tools for Generating and Analyzing Attack Graphs, vol. 3188, pp. 344–372 (11 2003). https://doi.org/10.1007/978-3-540-30101-1_17
32. Sood, A.K., Enbody, R.J.: Targeted cyberattacks: a superset of advanced persistent threats. IEEE Secur. Priv. 11(1), 54–61 (2013). https://doi.org/10.1109/MSP.2012.90
33. Spyridopoulos, T., Oikonomou, G., Tryfonas, T., Ge, M.: Game theoretic approach for cost-benefit analysis of malware proliferation prevention. In: Janczewski, L.J., Wolfe, H.B., Shenoi, S. (eds.) SEC 2013. IAICT, vol. 405, pp. 28–41. Springer, Heidelberg (2013). https://doi.org/10.1007/978-3-642-39218-4_3
34. Zakaria, W.Z.A., Abdollah, M.F., Mohd, O., Ariffin, A.F.M.: The rise of ransomware. In: Proceedings of the 2017 International Conference on Software and e-Business, pp. 66–70 (2017)
35. Zantua, M.A., Popovsky, V., Endicott-Popovsky, B., Holt, F.B.: Discovering a profile for protect and defend: penetration testing. In: Zaphiris, P., Ioannou, A. (eds.) LCT 2018. LNCS, vol. 10925, pp. 530–540. Springer, Cham (2018). https://doi.org/10.1007/978-3-319-91152-6_41

Author Index

Printed in the United States
by Baker & Taylor Publisher Services